CREATING YC...

ENTREPRENEURSHIP AND CAREERS
HOW TO MAKE A REAL DIFFERENCE AND SUCCEED IN A RADICALLY CHANGING WORLD

MEGATRENDS
YOUR PRODUCTS
NEW BUSINESSES
THOUGHT LEADERSHIP
MARKET RESEARCH
NEW MARKETING
TOP CAREERS

rialto

2015 WINNERS: Transition Coaching
Consultant of the Year. Business &
Leadership Transformation Speialists - UK.

DAVID L. WILLDEN

We at Rialto Consultancy have been helping thousands of leaders and hundreds of businesses to succeed throughout Europe since 2004. We help executives to become great leaders and to advance their careers and assist businesses to experience breakthroughs from the strengths of their people. We love what we do. It is indeed our "sweet spot." Some of the awards we have received include:

- UK Business & Leadership Transition Specialists – Winner 2015
- UK Transition Coaching Consultant of the Year – Winner 2014 & 2015
- England Transition Coaching Consultant of the Year – Winner 2014
- Outstanding Organization of the Year (SME)
- CIPD People Management Award 2013
- HR Distinction Award 2014

We were thrilled when David Willden published **Creating You, Inc**. Based on our experiences, the book's insights are powerful and desperately needed. Couple the book with great coaching and the right tools, you will be equipped to embark on a life-changing journey to discover your sweet-spot. One you are truly passionate about, one where there is an important and motivating need, and one that leverages your strengths and where you can really excel.

Careers and business are quickly changing. **Creating You, Inc.** will help you to understand important trends that are redefining the economy. You will learn how to develop a plan for yourself to become a known expert or thought-leader within your niche. You will understand how to research, develop, and market your own products and services to help you become a successful thought-leader in your niche.

If you would like to create a bright career for yourself, this book is a must read. It is never too late or too early to create a better life for yourself. Your career plays a significant role in how you feel about yourself and who you become.

Richard Chiumento

Director of Rialto Consultancy

COPYRIGHT

CONTENTS

INTRODUCTION

Creating You, Inc. is a guidebook designed to help you become successful in your career or business. It doesn't matter if you are just starting your career, in the middle of your career, or toward the tail end of your career. We believe you can choose at any time to create a career for yourself that deeply inspires you; one where you can make a real difference, one that helps you to develop deep connections with others, one where you can increase your chances of succeeding financially.

This guidebook helps you to:

1. **Discover Your Ideal Sweet Spot**—to help optimize your contributions and success.
2. **Understand Trends Redefining the World**—to help you identify and understand challenges and opportunities.
3. **Learn Powerful New Keys to Business Success**—to help improve your chances of starting, growing, or being a part of a successful business.
4. **See What Careers will be in High Demand.**
5. **Plan to Become a Thought Leader**—so you can become a major contributor in your field, innovate, and grow your business.
6. **Conduct Market Research to Find Opportunities**—to help you discover niches, products, and services to possibly focus on.
7. **Develop Your Compelling Thought Leader Products and Services**—to help you make a real difference and establish your business.
8. **Discover How to Market Your Products and Services in Today's World.**

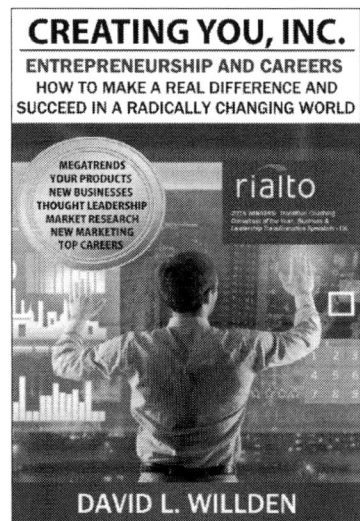

HOW TO READ THIS GUIDEBOOK

The best way to optimize your success is to use this guidebook as a source of information that helps you to think, to research, to plan, and to succeed and make a real difference in your career or business.

Request for Your Customer Review

It would mean a lot to me if you could provide a customer review on Amazon. Please click to access the book on Amazon to add a customer review.

ABOUT THE AUTHOR

David's greatest passion is in helping people to discover and create their own career or business. He also enjoys helping organizations to reinvent themselves and to develop and implement compelling strategies. He has led initiatives that have generated over $300 million in results.

David is currently the CEO of Breakthrough Practices, LLC; a firm that provides strategy, high performance transformation, employee engagement, and career consulting services. David is also a Senior Director at **RIALTO CONSULTANCY**; the top UK award winning international business and leadership transformational firm in London. Rialto has helped thousands of leaders and hundreds of businesses to succeed through Europe since 2004. Rialto has found their sweet spot and helps executives to become great leaders and to advance their careers and assist businesses to experience breakthroughs from the strengths of their people.

David has worked as a senior management adviser to top government officials and consulted extensively with federal organizations, Fortune 100 companies, small-medium sized businesses, and non-profit organizations. He has also worked as an executive for Larry H. Miller (owner of 100+ businesses, including Utah Jazz NBA team), Cap Gemini Consulting, and Franklin Covey where he led business turnarounds, managed 100+ consultants, and managed 100+ concurrent product development & other project teams.

David chaired and inaugurated World Strategy Week 2014—that brought together top strategy thought leaders, executives, and professionals from around the world. He is also on the Board of Directors for the Association of Strategic Planning focused on reinvention and marketing.

David has a M.S. from Johns Hopkins University and a B.A. from Brigham Young University.

1. How to Create a Successful Career of Purpose

How to create a career of purpose doing what you are most passionate about and where you can make a real difference

Prisoners at Work and Slaves to a Paycheck

You and I spend the prime of our lives and the prime of our days focused on making a living. What most people fail to recognize is just how much their work plays a significant role in how they feel about themselves and the kind of person they become. What you focus on to make a living is ultimately important to your physical, emotional, mental, and spiritual well-being.

According to an ongoing study by Gallup involving over 25 million employees in 195 different countries, only 13% of employees are engaged in their jobs. That means that only one in eight workers feel they are making a positive contribution and are committed to their job and organization. Sixty-three percent of employees are not engaged in their jobs. In other words, they have "checked out." They are not motivated. They do their jobs, but not with passion and energy. Twenty-four percent of the workforce is actively disengaged. These workers are extremely unhappy at work. They are even hostile to their organizations. There are almost twice as many employees who are actively disengaged as there are employees who are engaged in their jobs. Gallup estimates that the cost of active disengagement within the U.S. alone is between $450 to $550 billion dollars per year.[1]

Few things are worse than feeling like you are a prisoner at work and are a slave to a paycheck. It is miserable being in a political and cut throat environment where no one genuinely cares about you. It is frustrating and even painful when your opinions don't matter. It isn't helpful when you struggle in seeing any real meaningful purpose in your organization. Being in such an environment is toxic to how you feel about yourself and the kind of person you want to become. Many times, we simply hang-on, hoping for a better future. The unfortunate truth is that *if you wait and hope that your career will improve with your current employer, the probability is that it won't.*

Let me ask you some important questions. Are you worn out with being in a miserable environment? Are you emotionally drained from the frustration and pain of feeling that your opinions really don't matter? How can you feel good about yourself in a toxic environment? I'm not suggesting that you just quit your job. What I am suggesting is that you plan for a brighter future and then work intelligently to make that plan a reality.

Two of the Most Powerful Motivations that Lead to Change

Research shows that those who are most successful in overcoming addictive behaviors are those who are internally motivated to change (e.g., see long-term consequences of their behaviors) and who have found something they are truly passionate about and that deeply motivates them (e.g., fulfilling relationships, spiritual strength, a new career).

The two most powerful motivators that move all of us to improve and succeed are pain and happiness. This seems basic and so simple in theory, but few tap into these motivational forces successfully to help them succeed and enjoy a happier life.

Our nature as humans is to ignore, deny, or refuse to think about pain. We hope and we pretend that the future will be better—even though we aren't sure what we want and how to get there. We often ignore or sometimes even deny the future impact of our current actions and circumstances because it is too uncomfortable or even painful for us to think about. Putting our head in the sand doesn't work.

Both pain and happiness are intended to help you. Careful thought and reason are powerful; however, alone they can't lead us to the results we desire.

Pain is a powerful motivator. It can be a blessing if you use it right. Pain helps us from seriously hurting ourselves. It tells us when we have a sickness or injury that needs treatment. It teaches us important lessons. It motivates problem-solving, creativity, and resourcefulness. It helps us to develop empathy for others. Most importantly, pain can motivate us to change and to become better.

A dream of happiness can be the most powerful motivator if we allow ourselves to tap deeply into it. It can deeply inspire you. The right vision of hope and happiness is one that deeply resonates with your soul in a way that you can't fully explain to others. It is a vision that becomes so real that you can see it, you can hear it, and you can feel it. It is a vision so powerful that it indeed motivates you to action and to improve.

So, how can you fully tap into these powerful motivators to help you succeed?

Let's start with pain. When we associate massive pain to a potential outcome, we avoid it at all costs. It is easy to not think about the outcomes of our current direction. But, if you do, it can bless you. Take the time to think about where you are headed and what the results will look like. The clearer you can paint a picture in your mind of the outcome, the more vivid and real it will be for you. The more descriptive you can be about the pain you see and feel, and the more it will influence you.

Please think about the questions below and write down your responses:

- What will the future look like if there isn't a change?
- What does it look like?
- What does it feel like?

To have a vision of the pain we will experience if we do not change is powerful, but it is not enough motivation to sustain the growth we need and want. A vision of happiness is what can inspire and sustain us in the long-term. It is something that we are willing to sacrifice and dedicate ourselves to.

Please begin to create a vision of happiness for yourself. Think about the questions below and write down your responses:

- What does your vision of happiness look like?
- What does it feel like?
- When thinking of your future career, what would it look and feel like if you focused on something where you could really make a difference?

Determine to Become an Agent for Yourself

How many cynics have robbed people of dreams that could have been realities? Do not allow yourself to be a victim to the limited mindsets of others and even yourself.

We each have written programs in our hearts and minds about ourselves. These programs tell us who we can become and who we cannot become. Our internal programs are impacted by the experiences we have and they too often try and tell us who we are and should be. Often, it is the negative experiences that we remember most. For instance, you may remember and feel anger, sorrow, and hurt from how you were treated. You may have been a victim of hate and physical, mental, and/or emotional abuse. You can't allow these experiences to define you. Instead, you can look at how these experiences helped you to become more understanding and compassionate of others.

It is often these programs or beliefs about ourselves that hold us back and need to be reprogrammed.

The most powerful lesson that you can learn is that you *can* choose to be your own agent for change and not a victim. You literally *can* become the kind of person you want to become. This is not only your privilege, but I believe it *is your right and responsibility to create your future.*

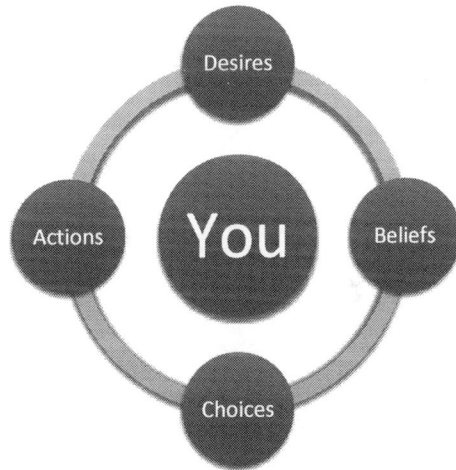

Desires

Actions

You

Beliefs

Choices

You may want to memorize this powerful truth, burn it into your soul, and remind yourself frequently of its importance. *As you continue to carry within your heart and mind a vision of who you desire to become, your capacity to make that vision a reality will grow daily. Your persistent desires and beliefs determine who you become. What you desire impacts your choices. Your choices lead to actions. Together, your desires, beliefs, choices, and actions determine who you become.*

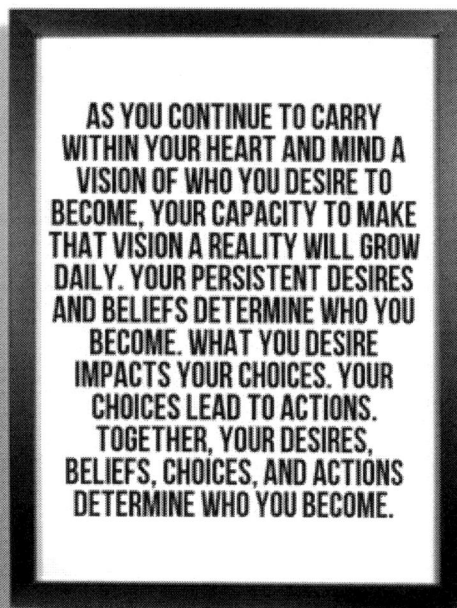

> AS YOU CONTINUE TO CARRY WITHIN YOUR HEART AND MIND A VISION OF WHO YOU DESIRE TO BECOME, YOUR CAPACITY TO MAKE THAT VISION A REALITY WILL GROW DAILY. YOUR PERSISTENT DESIRES AND BELIEFS DETERMINE WHO YOU BECOME. WHAT YOU DESIRE IMPACTS YOUR CHOICES. YOUR CHOICES LEAD TO ACTIONS. TOGETHER, YOUR DESIRES, BELIEFS, CHOICES, AND ACTIONS DETERMINE WHO YOU BECOME.

Please return back to your vision that you began to work on and ask yourself these follow-up questions:

- What beliefs about yourself and others do you want to have?
- What limiting beliefs about yourself and others do you want to eliminate?
- How can you successfully reprogram your beliefs so that you can succeed?

Renew Daily

It is easy to slip back into our old mindsets and habits. Too often, we allow ourselves to slip into a cycle of self-pity and anger. One of the simplest and most effective ways to overcome these inclinations is to do one simple thing. Make time every day to renew; to remind yourself of your vision. Make it a point to diligently search how you can achieve the vision you desire, become the kind of person you want, and develop the right kind of action plans that will get you there. Each time you do this, you are making your dream that much more of a reality. It is becoming more and more etched in to your soul.

As you do this on a regular basis, you begin to create a momentum of success.

The World Desperately Needs You

What the world desperately needs are people who understand the challenges and opportunities ahead, hold and cherish high values, have courage to stand for what is right, and are willing to develop the capacities needed to address the challenges.

Start with Your Noble Passions

The best thing you can do to make a real difference is to identify and focus on your most noble of passions. In fact, the more noble passions you acquire, the better you will be able to help others. I will discuss this topic in more detail in the next chapter and will ask questions to help you find those passions.

You and I have an urge and need to find and live a life of meaning. Viktor Frankl lived in Nazi concentration camps. He was a surgeon and a psychiatrist. He believed that the young, strong, and healthy would be the ones who would survive the horrors of the camp. While in the camps, Viktor interviewed and helped his fellow prisoners. What he learned was that the key to survival was not youth, strength, or health. This surprised him. Those that did survive shared a common strength. *They all had something to live for. They had meaning in their life.* This insight changed Viktor's life.

Viktor wrote "the men who walked through the huts comforting others; giving away their last piece of bread. They may have been few in number, but they offer sufficient proof that everything can be taken from a man, but one thing: the last of human freedoms —to choose one's own attitude in any given set of circumstances—to choose one's own way."[2]

Frankl survived the incredible ordeals and humiliation of the Nazi camps by dedicating himself to helping other prisoners develop their sense of purpose and to avoid suicides—which were common. Frankl held on to his vision of one day being reunited with his wife and of standing in front of a classroom again and teaching the powerful lessons he was learning.

Courage

It takes courage to dream and then to make our dreams a reality. We each face fears, stress, and anxieties. It takes courage to become who you want to become. It takes courage to help create a positive future for the world. Courage doesn't just happen, it is developed. Courage is mental and emotional preparedness. It is the ability to confront fear, pain, intimidations, and danger.

As we develop our courage, we become stronger. It takes real courage to overcome the fear of being rejected by others who may intentionally or even unintentionally be dragging us down.

Winston Churchill struggled in school and failed the sixth grade. He suffered defeat in multiple political elections. He felt very alone. He saw what Hitler was doing and tried warning others about Nazi Germany. No one wanted to listen. Winston's warnings put him out of favor with the people. The people wanted to ignore what Hitler and Mussolini were doing.

Neville Chamberlain, the Prime Minister before Winston Churchill, seemed to want to simply appease Germany's Hitler and Italy's Mussolini. Neville was determined to avoid war no matter what it took. The British people supported Chamberlain. It meant less pain, less sacrifice, less worry, and more of the same—or so they hoped. Consequently, despite the danger signals, the British were not prepared as they should have been for war and suffered tremendous consequences—over 450,000 causalities.

At the ripe old age of 62, Winston Churchill finally became the Prime Minister. Winston refused to consider defeat during World War II. This was extremely difficult in the early days of the war when Britain stood alone. And, despite the fear of his own speech impediment, it was Churchill's courage and his speeches and radio broadcasts that kept the British people inspired until victory was won over Nazi Germany.

Winston taught that *"courage is the first human quality because it is the quality which will guarantee all others."*

Create Hope in Yourself — Despite Your Trials

Trials and difficulties can seem like curses, but they can prepare us with the grit needed to really help others. Consider the example of Abraham. He was born dirt-poor. His schooling was very limited. He had no choice, but to toil hard to support the family. His mother was a deeply religious person and she impressed upon him the importance of education.

Abraham's mother died when he was nine years old and his sister Sarah was eleven. They were heartbroken. To make matters worse, during these hard times, they were left alone for several months. Their father left the children to find a new wife. Abraham and his sister thought they were abandoned. When their father returned, he brought with him his new wife and her children. Abraham desperately needed love and when he first met his new mother, he rushed up to her and buried his face in her skirt. He loved his step-mother. She loved him dearly and supported and encouraged him in his love of learning as best as circumstances would allow.

When he was 21, Abraham moved away from home and worked to haul freight, worked as a shopkeeper, and as a postmaster. He was a business partner in the shop and unfortunately, the business failed—and he spent years paying off the debt. He decided to start a business later on and failed again. During this time, he decided to try and run for public office, but lost.

Abraham fell deeply in love. Unfortunately, his sweetheart died and this broke his heart. The pain was too much for him. He had been through too much. He had a nervous breakdown and was in bed for six months trying to recover.

Abraham continued to have a passion for learning, wanted to better his life, and hoped and believed he could make a difference. He had a friend who loaned him law books. He studied these books and he taught himself the law. He later took and passed the bar examination. This opened the door for him and he was able to work as an attorney. He developed a good reputation for being honest, courageous, and deeply valuing democracy and nationalism.

Abraham ran for office three times and lost each time, until he finally ran for congress and won one term, but lost the second term. He ran several more times for public office, losing each time.

Finally, Abraham ran for and won the highest office in the United States— the Presidency in 1860.

Abraham Lincoln led the nation during the bloodiest war in the history of the U.S—the Civil War. It was a time of political and moral crisis. Despite overwhelming pressures, he charted a course that abolished slavery and preserved the Union.

With the promise and relief of victory on the horizon, Abraham and Mary went to Ford's Theater to enjoy a comedy show. John Wilkes Booth slipped into the presidential box and shot Lincoln in the head.

Today, Abraham Lincoln is regarded as one of the most significant figures in the history of mankind.

Dedication to Constant Learning

A constant dedication to learning is key to being able to make a difference. Few imagined that Tom would amount to anything. He grew up in Ohio and was the last of seven children. His father, Samuel, had various vocations— e.g., splitting shingles for roofs, tailor, and tavern keeper. Samuel was also an exiled political activist who had escaped from Canada into the U.S. Tom's mother was a school teacher who died when Tom was 24 years old.

As a child, Tom was hyperactive and easily distracted. He went to public school for a total of twelve weeks. He was told he was "addled" or essentially too stupid to learn anything. Tom's mother pulled him out of school; determined to teach him herself. Her love and persistence inspired him to love learning. Her dedication to Tom deeply motivated him, gave him hope, and he determined that he would strive not to disappoint her. Tom credited his mother for believing in him when others didn't.

By the time Thomas was twelve, he had lost most of his hearing. Instead of getting discouraged with life, he continued to move forward.

Because of Thomas Edison's unrelenting dedication to learning and experimentation, he ended up acquiring 1,093 patents. His inventions included the phonograph, motion picture camera, and a long-lasting electric light bulb. Thomas Edison's discoveries changed the world.

Why "Now" is the Ideal Time to Create Your Future Career

Now is the best time to plan for your new future. Why waste your career doing something that you can't really be fully engaged in? I encourage you to determine not to waste the prime of your day and your life somewhere doing something that doesn't inspire you.

There is another reason you may want to begin to develop and implement a new plan for your future. Companies typically staff up with temps during a recovery and convert them to permanent workers as conditions improve. That hasn't been happening. According to an article in Forbes written by Elaine Pofeldt, "currently about 20-30% of the workforce in Fortune 100 companies is made up of 'contingent' workers: that percentage is expected to swell to 50% by 2020."[3] As of 2013, the number of temporary jobs rose more than 50 percent since the recession in 2009.

The use of temporary employees has expanded into all sectors (e.g., lawyers, doctors). U.S., Adecco predicts that the "rate of growth in contingent workers will be 3-4 times the growth rate of traditional jobs and will soon comprise at least 30% or more of the global workforce."[4]

Tammy Erickson, in a Harvard Business Review blog article titled "The Rise of the New Contract Worker" cited the benefits of contingent talent:

- **Cost flexibility**: companies don't need to invest in full-time employees.
- **Speed and agility**: getting the right talent to meet new needs.
- **Innovation**: new knowledge and fresh ideas.

These temporary employment trends are symptomatic of a more basic dynamic. Companies do not last as long. Fortune started tracking Fortune 500 companies in 1955. Of the 500 companies on that list, only 71 were still there in 2008. Also, "a full one-third of the companies listed in the 1979 Fortune 500 had vanished by 1983..."[5]

It is not certain that this trend toward temporary and contract work will continue. Unless businesses and the economy stabilize, however, this trend will likely continue. One thing is certain. To assume the economic environment will be the same as when our fathers or grandfathers had long-term and even life-time jobs—isn't wise. It is estimated that workers today between the ages of 21 to 31 will likely have between 12 to 15 jobs.

2. How to Discover Your Ideal Sweet Spot

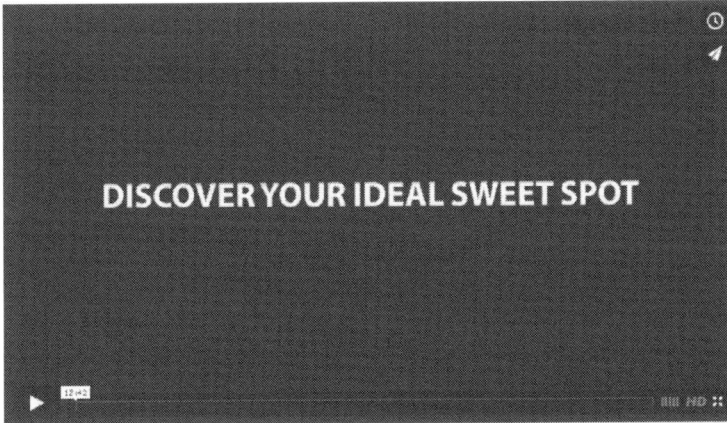

DISCOVER YOUR IDEAL SWEET SPOT

http://creating-you-inc.com/book-videos/

There are four key important considerations to examine to help you make your optimal business or career decision:

- Who do you want to become?
- What are your noble passions?
- What are your natural talents and strengths?
- Where are there needs and opportunities?

When you find a niche that aligns with each of the four critical factors above—you are discovering your ideal sweet spot.

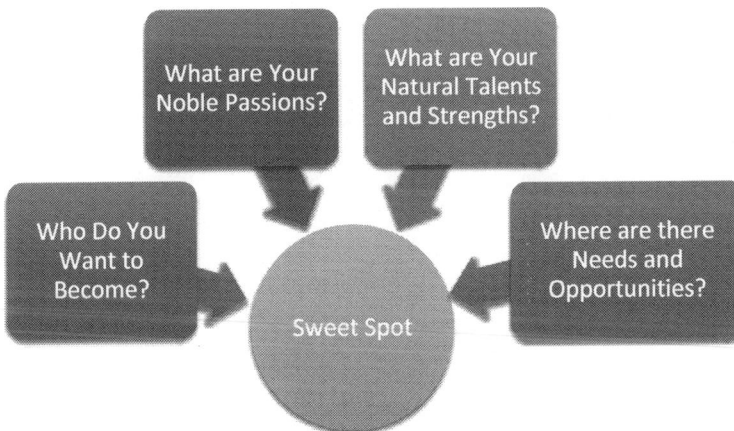

WHO DO YOU WANT TO BECOME?

Today, most people believe that who they are is fixed or set. In other words, their intellect, personality, talents, and other traits are unchangeable. Furthermore, they believe they are simply a by-product of the environment, genetics, or fate. This is understandable and regrettable. For many years, scientists chased after theories that our physical characteristics are set and define who we are. In fact, during the 20th century, there was consensus among neuroscientists that the brain was relatively unchangeable after childhood. Rigorous research proved otherwise. Neuroplasticity has replaced the belief that the brain is a physiologically static organ. We know that our brains change throughout our lives. Studies prove that changes and experiences can alter the brain's anatomy and physiology.

We can become who we truly desire if we do the right things to become the person we hope to be. There are a myriad of excuses we can use to keep from becoming who we desire. The truth is that you and I know the keys. The real reason that may be holding us back is that we may not fully see and feel the pain of our current trajectory. Our desire or vision of who we hope to become may not be strong and persistent enough. Mistaken beliefs about our limits may be holding us back. It may be that we are not disciplined enough to follow-up on actions we need to take.

Your ability to create a better future is a function of your desires, beliefs, choices, and actions. For good or evil, you determine who you become. Becoming the person you desire is not a function of chance. The key to your ability to become who you desire is to understand and adopt universal truths or natural laws. By understanding natural laws, you begin to understand the laws of cause and effect.

James Allen, the British philosophical writer wrote, "A noble and Godlike character is not a thing of favor or chance, but it is the natural result of continued effort in right thinking; the effect of long-cherished association with Godlike thoughts." He says that, "Ignoble and bestial character, by the same process, is the result of the continued harboring of groveling thoughts." He continues, "Of all the beautiful truths pertaining to the soul, which have been restored and brought to light in this age, none is more gladdening or fruitful of divine promise and confidence than this—that man is the master of thought, the molder of character, and maker and shaper of condition, environment, and destiny."

James emphasized that, "When he (man) begins to reflect upon his condition, and to **search diligently for the Law upon which his being is established, he then becomes the wise master**, directing his energies with intelligence, and fashioning his thoughts to fruitful issues. Such is the conscious master that man can only thus become by discovering within himself the laws of thought, which discovery is totally a matter of application, self-analysis, and experience."[6] This law or absolute truth governs the universe.

Develop Clarity and Capability

Remember that what the world desperately needs is people who understand the challenges and opportunities ahead, hold and cherish high values, have courage to stand for what is right, and are willing to develop the capacity to address the challenges.
Determine that you will become extremely capable in an area that can significantly help others.

As you find your ideal sweet spot and develop and maintain a powerful vision for yourself, your anxieties and worries will increasingly disappear and be replaced with hope and ultimately, the realization that your dreams will come true.

As you develop clarity on who you want to become, what you stand for, where you want to go, and how you will get there, you will develop a growing sense of stability.

Questions

- What kind of person do you deeply desire to become?
- What do you really want to contribute?
- Is this desire strong enough that it can help to guide your choices and actions?
- How can you become that better person?
- What is the best way to get there?
- What could hold you back?
- What can you do to overcome the obstacles?

WHAT ARE YOUR MOST NOBLE PASSIONS?

By focusing on your most noble passions, you increase the chances that you will become the kind of person you yearn to become.

As we learned, Viktor Frankl found that those who survived the horrors of the Nazi concentration camps weren't the young, strong, and healthy. They were those that had meaning in their life. Viktor himself survived by helping others find their purpose in living.

To learn more about noble passions, let's go back in time and look briefly at George Washington. On June 15, 1775, he had just been commissioned as commander-in-chief of the Continental Army—just two days after the Boston siege. To outsiders, this appointment could have been seen as an honor. George wrote to his wife Martha saying, "far from seeking this appointment, I have used every endeavor in my power to avoid it, not only from my unwillingness to part with you and the family, but from a consciousness of its being a trust too great for my capacity....it has been a kind of destiny that has thrown me upon this service."[7]

George was nervous and worried—for good reason. George Washington had been retired from military life for fifteen years, during which he had not even drilled a militia company. His only prior experience had been in backwoods warfare—a very different kind of warfare—and most notably in the Braddock campaign of 1755, which had been a disaster. He had never led an army in battle, never before commanded anything larger than a regiment, and never had he directed a siege.[8]

General Washington knew he wasn't prepared to take on the impossible assignment of leading the Continental Army to victory. He probably had a realistic idea of how immense that responsibility would be. For such a trust, to lead an undisciplined, poorly armed volunteer force of farmers and tradesmen against the best-trained, best-equipped, most formidable military on earth—and with so much riding on the outcome—was, in reality, more than any man was qualified for.

What would have happened if George Washington would have declined, ran away from, or approached his responsibilities without hope and faith in a brighter future? There is no question that he wanted to be with his family and on his beautiful and peaceful farm at Mount Vernon. Why sacrifice everything?

George Washington decided to focus on the most noble of his passions. He chose to focus on helping a young country to provide and protect the privileges of life, liberty, and the pursuit of happiness.

The whole world could be a different place today if George Washington had shirked his responsibility. Instead of enjoying the blessings of democracy, we may still be the victims of aristocracies, caste systems, or autocracies.

The World Needs You

The world desperately needs you, whether or not you know it or they know it. The world desperately needs people who understand the challenges and opportunities ahead. It needs people who hold and cherish high values and who focus on noble passions. It needs people who have courage to stand for what is right and are willing to develop the capacity to address challenges.

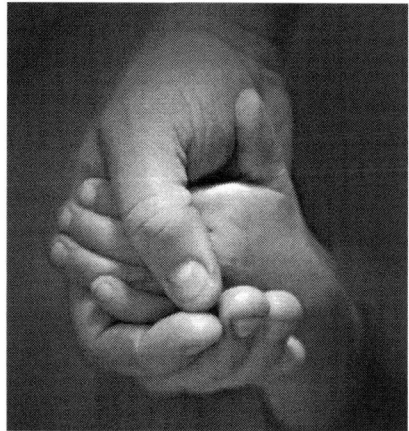

Noble passions stem from our deepest values and are what can motivate us most. To be noble is to possess high moral principles and ideals. A passion is an intense emotion or enthusiasm for something. To have a noble passion is to have a strong emotion for a cause that builds others. Passions focused on integrity, honoring, and building others are constructive and noble. Noble passions are based on genuine love. They strengthen, elevate, and help others. They inspire others to enjoy more happiness, to be more compassionate, and become more capable.

Passion focused on personal fame, wealth, and selfish indulgences can be damaging. Passions that deprive others of their honor, dignity, and freedom are destructive. Selfish passions are ego based, competitive, controlling, degrading, focused on damaging short-term pleasures, manipulative, and dishonest.

Why focus on noble passions?

By focusing on your noble passions, you'll find greater joy. You will better understand who you are and can become more courageous and willing to make meaningful sacrifices that will improve the lives of others.

What are your noble passions?

- What noble passions touch your heart most?
- What hurts your soul most?
- What are the biggest problems that you like to help solve?
- What passion are you most willing to sacrifice for?
- If you could dedicate your life to helping and building others, what would you do?
- How motivated would you be to spend the remainder of your life dedicated to this cause?

HOW TO DISCOVER YOUR TALENTS

Tom Rath wrote in StrengthFinder 2.0 that, "Unfortunately, most of us have little sense of our talents and strengths, much less the ability to build our lives around them. Instead, guided by our parents, by our teachers, by our managers, and by psychology's fascination with pathology, we become experts in our weaknesses and spend our lives trying to repair these flaws while our strengths lie dormant and neglected."[9]

Peter Drucker, a management consultant, educator, and author, whose writings contributed to the philosophical and practical foundations of the modern business corporation said, "Most Americans do not know what their strengths are. When you ask them, they look at you with a blank stare or they respond in terms of subject knowledge, which is the wrong answer."[10]

Each of us has talents that we can discover and develop. Each person's talents are enduring and unique. Our greatest potential for growth is in the area of his or her greatest strength. When developed and used, a talent can bring us deep fulfillment and joy.

What is a Talent and Why is it Important?

A talent is an innate ability and a blessing you have that allows you to do something with little or no practice, training, or experience. Usually, talents come so easily to us that we don't recognize them as talents. We assume everyone can do the same things.

Tom Rath and Gallup defined a talent differently. They said it is a "naturally recurring pattern of thought, feeling, or behavior that can be productively applied."[11]

Turning a Talent into a Strength

A talent is turned into a strength as it is developed. Strength is developed as one gains knowledge and experience. This diagram suggests talent constitutes 50% of a person's capability in a given area. Experience, along with knowledge, constitutes the other 50%.

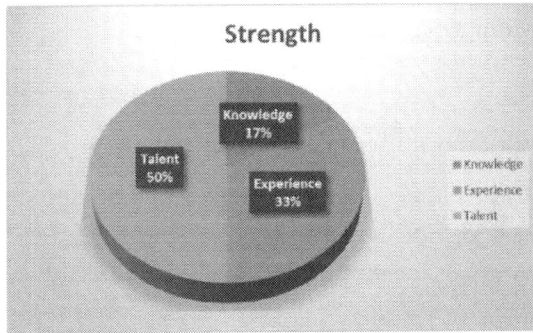

Another way of looking at strength is as follows:

Talent + Knowledge x Experience = Strength

- **Talent**: A talent is an innate ability and gift you have that allows you to do something with little or no practice, training, or experience.
- **Knowledge**: The wisdom needed to excel in an area.
- **Experience**: The application of knowledge.
- **Strength**: To be outstanding at something.

Talent Inventory Questions

- What noble yearnings do you have?
- What topics and/or skills do you learn quickly and thoroughly love learning?
- What types of things give you the most joy and sense of fulfillment?
- Are there things that you love doing so much that you easily lose track of time when you are doing them? What are they?
- What natural abilities do you have today?

Strengths Inventory Questions

- Which of your natural talents do you believe you've built into strengths?
- How can you fully develop and leverage your natural talents so that you can grow and contribute exponentially?
- What is your plan to do this?

REMEMBER THAT TALENTS AND STRENGTHS ARE NOT SET

Our talents and strengths can also become a source of weakness for us if we become arrogant or prideful about ourselves. How many celebrities have we seen who started their careers humble and grateful, but later turned into narcissistic monsters?

Some people take talent too far—as though they are fixed. As we have learned, you and I are not fixed mentally, emotionally, spiritually, or physically. We know that changes and experiences can alter our brains' anatomy and physiology.

Interestingly, our weaknesses can become our strengths. Why is this? It is because our desire to develop in an area may grow significantly. Also, when we are weak at something, we are humbler and more willing to dig in and learn. We can choose to be more determined to turn the perceived weakness into strength.

Carol S. Dweck, Ph.D. is a well-known Professor at Stanford University and one of the leading researchers in the field of motivation. Carol earned her Ph.D. from Yale University and taught at Columbia University, Harvard University, and the University of Illinois before coming to Stanford. In her research, she found students that have a belief that their intelligence is fixed, spend more time trying to look smart and avoid at any cost looking dumb. These students struggle. They dread failure because it shows what their limitations are as a human being. They avoid situations that stretch and challenge them. Students, on the other hand, that have a growth mindset, believe that their talents and strengths can be developed through effort, good teaching, and persistence. Students with a growth mindset are happier and are more likely to continue at something, despite setbacks.[12]

Persistent desires and beliefs lead to choices and actions and ultimately mold our character. The following are well-known examples of people who succeeded, despite the fact that others felt that they didn't have enough talent to succeed in their occupation:

- Oprah Winfrey was fired from one of her first jobs because she was "unfit for TV."
- Walt Disney was fired by a newspaper editor because "He lacked imagination and had not good ideas."
- Before J.K. Rowling had any "Harry Potter" success, the writer was a divorced single mother on welfare struggling to get by while also attending school and writing a novel.
- Before landing "I Love Lucy," Lucille Ball was widely regarded as a failed actress.
- After his first audition, Sidney Poitier was told by the casting director, "Why don't you stop wasting peoples' time and go out and become a dishwasher or something?" Sidney went on to win an Oscar.
- Steven Spielberg was rejected from the University of Southern California, School of Theater, Film, and Television three times.
- Stephen King received 30 rejections for his book "Carrie." Today, King is one of the best-selling authors of all time and "Carrie" is on its second movie re-make.
- Michael Jordan was cut from his high school basketball team. "I have failed over and over and over again in my life. And that is why I succeed."
- Steve Jobs was a college dropout, a fired tech executive, and an unsuccessful businessman.

Talent Related Tools

The following are tools that you can use to help you find your talents and strengths.

Strengths Finder

To help people discover their talents, Gallup developed an online assessment tool. The assessment helps you to find which 5 of 34 possible themes best match you. To get access to the tool, you need to purchase a copy of **Strengthsfinder 2.0**. In addition to taking the online assessment, Gallup, in their own words below, suggests that you also consider:

- **Yearnings** can reveal the presence of a talent, particularly when they are felt early in life. A yearning can be described as an internal force, an almost magnetic attraction that leads you to a particular activity or environment time and again.
- **Rapid learning** reveals other traces of talent. In the context of a new challenge or a new environment, something sparks your talents. Immediately, your brain seems to light up as if a whole bank of switches were suddenly flicked "on"—and the speed at which you anticipate the steps of a new activity, acquire a new skill, or gain new knowledge provides a telltale clue to the talents' presence and power.
- **Satisfaction** is psychological fulfillment that results when you take on and successfully meet challenges that engage your greatest talents. Pay close attention to the situations that seem to bring you these energizing experiences. If you can identify them, you will be well on your way to pinpointing some of your dominant talents.
- **Timelessness** also can serve as a clue to talent. If you have ever become so engrossed in an activity that you lost all track of time, it may have been because the activity engaged you at a deep, natural level—the level of great talent.
- **Glimpses of excellence** are flashes of outstanding performance that have been observed by you or others. In these moments, the task at hand has tapped some of your greatest talents and directly displayed your potential for strength.[13]

Discover Your Strengths

- The website FreeStrengthsTest.Workuno.com offers free online assessments to help you discover your strengths.

Myers-Briggs Personality Test

The Myers-Briggs Type Indicator assessment is a questionnaire that measures preferences in how people perceive the world and make decisions.

What's Your Personality Type?

Use the questions on the outside of the chart to determine the four letters of your Myers-Briggs type.
For each pair of letters, choose the side that seems most natural to you, even if you don't agree with every description.

- Click for information on the test
- Click for free version of assessment
- Click for common careers for personality types

Hermann Brain Dominance Instrument

The Hermann Brain Dominance Instrument is a system designed to measure and describe thinking preferences in people.

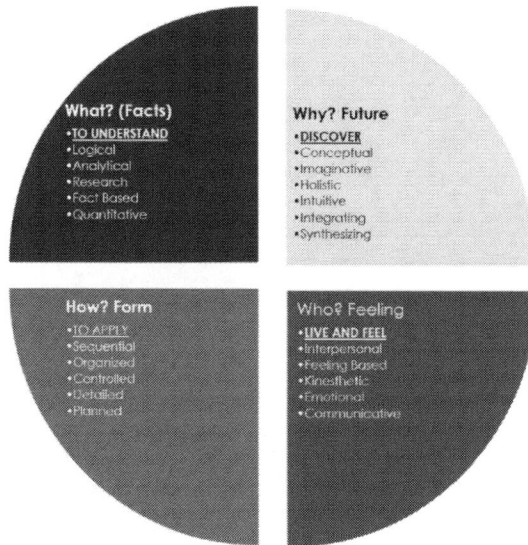

There are four thinking preferences

- What do you believe is your most dominant color?
- What is your second most dominant color?
- Third?

Link to more information

360 Degree Input

Getting input from others on your strengths can be especially helpful. Reachcc.com offers a 15 day free trial tool that allows you to send out requests to a large number of people to provide you anonymous input. People identify which attributes, skills, strengths, and weaknesses best characterize you.

3. TRENDS REDEFINING THE WORLD

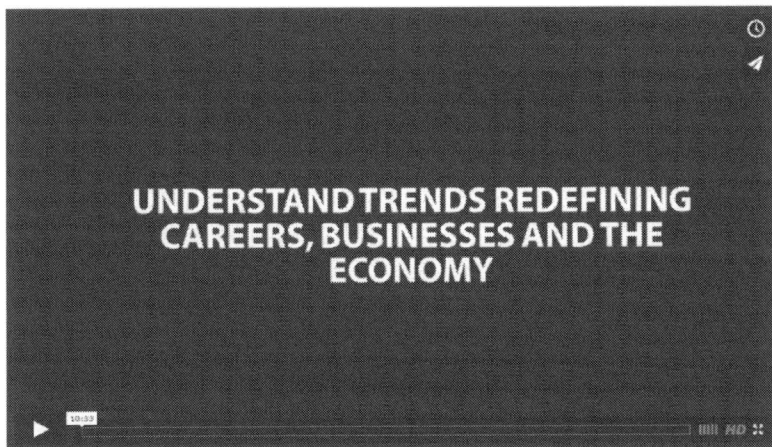

UNDERSTAND TRENDS REDEFINING CAREERS, BUSINESSES AND THE ECONOMY

http://creating-you-inc.com/book-videos/

There are abundant opportunities for those who are willing to look to the future and act. Your success will depend largely on your ability to gather reliable information, objectively review the information, anticipate outcomes, take action, and in influencing others.

Consider Jeff Bezos. In 1994, he quit his high paying SVP job with D.E. Shaw & Co.— a hedge fund company. He had learned about the rapid growth of the internet. He knew where the internet was headed and decided the risk was worth it. So, he and his wife drove from New York to Seattle and started Amazon in his garage.

As of 2014, Amazon is the largest online retailer and the ninth overall largest retailer. Jeff's net worth is $30.7 billion dollars. Jeff Bezos continues to say that "this is day 1 for the internet. We still have so much more to learn."

In this chapter, I provide rich megatrends and game-changing trends that you will want to carefully review. Under each megatrend or game-changing trend, look for the paragraph titled "Needs and Opportunities to Consider." Ask yourself the question, "is this something I should focus on?" As you review these trends, I encourage you to write down the ideas, thoughts, and feelings you have. Writing is a powerful way to reflect, to capture feelings, to develop ideas, and to refine your thinking.

Preparing for the Future is Vital

Understanding, preparing for, and creating a positive future is vital. Most people don't think about, let alone prepare for, the imminent future, even when dangers or opportunities are right in front of them.

What 9/11 Taught Us

Consider the September 11, 2001 attacks on New York City and Virginia by 19 terrorists associated with al-Qaeda. Two planes were flown into the twin towers of the World Trade Center in New York City. A third plane hit the Pentagon just outside of Washington D.C. A fourth plane crashed in a field in Pennsylvania. The attacks resulted in the deaths of 2,996 people including more than 400 police and firefighters. The attacks also had a horrific effect on the global markets, possibly resulting in trillions of dollars of damage.

What surprised the U.S. was that it was not engaged in any foreign wars at the time. Conflicts always happened outside of the U.S. and not within it. How could this happen within the U.S. people wondered? Hysteria and worry gripped the nation and safety and vigilance became a top priority.

Massive changes were made in government organizations. New policies such as the USA Patriot Act put national security and defense as top priorities, even above civil liberties. Since 9/11, the U.S. has been involved in major wars in Afghanistan and Iraq.

The Inspector General for the CIA, Senate, House committees, and a special 9/11 Commission reviewed the circumstances surrounding the 9/11 attacks and the level of preparedness of the U.S. The reports were not positive!

The 9/11 Commission wrote:

> The 9/11 attacks were a shock, but they should not have
> come as a surprise. Islamist extremists had given plenty of
> warning that they meant to kill Americans indiscriminately
> and in large numbers. Although Osama Bin Laden himself
> would not emerge as a signal threat until the late 1990's, the
> threat of Islamist terrorism grew over the decade.

To sum it up, the 9/11 Commission also wrote, "We believe the 9/11
attacks revealed four kinds of failures: in imagination, policy,
capabilities, and management."[14]

**Developing the ability to look to the future, gather reliable
information, analyze the information, and determine what actions
to take is vital to your success.**

KEY MEGATRENDS AND OTHER CRITICAL TRENDS YOU NEED TO KNOW ABOUT

A megatrend is at the root of other smaller trends and it is what drives the others. A megatrend is generally unstoppable. It leads to profound and wide reaching changes. It is so massive that it figuratively moves mountains, cities,

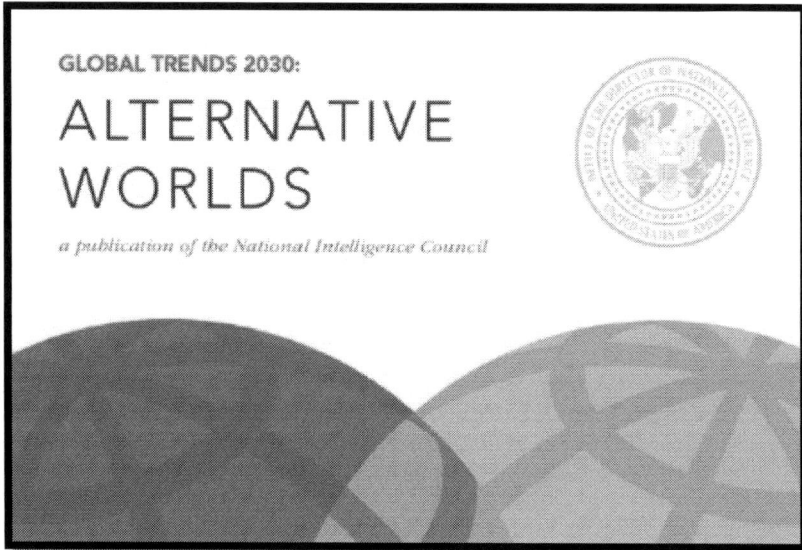

GLOBAL TRENDS 2030:

ALTERNATIVE WORLDS

a publication of the National Intelligence Council

and continents.

Some of the megatrends that we will review offer the hope of a better world. Others are dangerous and could destroy mankind.

We will focus on the "Spread of Democracy" as well as the megatrends and game-changers identified by the National Intelligence Council (NIC). Every four years, the NIC facilitates the development of a "Global Trends" report. In generating these reports, the NIC conducts conferences, workshops, and individual meetings with scholars, experts, universities, think tanks, science labs, businesses, and government institutions from around the world. Their objective is to detect and anticipate future trends. These reports are used by the White House, US Intelligence Community, other government entities, educational institutions, businesses, and non-profit organizations for planning purposes.

In NIC's most recent Global Trends 2030 report, they identified four megatrends. They include: 1. Individual Empowerment. 2. Diffusion of Power. 3. Demographic Patterns. 4. Food, Water, and the Energy Nexus.

NIC also identified six game-changers. Game-changers are not as certain as megatrends; although, the probability of their occurrence is high. More importantly, the impact of the game-changers is high. The six game-changers include: 1. Crisis-Prone Global Economy. 2. The Governance Gap. 3. The Potential for Increased Conflict. 4. Wider Scope of Regional Instability. 5. The Impact of New Technologies. 6. The Role of the United States.[15]

List of Megatrends and Game-Changers We Will Review

Megatrends

1. Spreading of Democracy.
2. Individual Empowerment.
3. Diffusion of Power.
4. Demographic Patterns.
5. Growing Food, Water, and Energy Needs.

Game-Changers

1. Crisis-Prone Global Economy.
2. The Governance Gap.
3. The Potential for Increased Conflict.
4. Wider Scope of Regional Instability.
5. The Role of the United States.
6. The Impact of New Technologies.

I will expand beyond what the technologies that NIC identifies and focus on additional high impact technologies.

THE SPREAD OF DEMOCRACY

We are just beginning to see the impact of the spread of democracy. Freedom touches and addresses one of the deepest and most profound hungers that we have as humans. The small experiment of freedom in the United States drastically changed the world. Now, democracy is spreading throughout the world.

The spread of democracy is an exciting change from the past. It is changing economies, political structures, cultures, and the basic fabric of societies. Today, there are 196 countries in the world. The democracy index measures the state of democracy in 167 of those countries. According to the index, 24 countries in North America and Western Europe are considered to be full democracies. Twenty-one countries in Latin America and the Caribbean are considered to be "flawed democracies." One hundred countries in Asia, Australasia, Central and Eastern Europe, and the Sub-Saharan Africa are considered to be hybrid regimes. Twenty countries are authoritarian regimes.[16]

Changes Throughout the World

In June of 1988, while I was eagerly waiting to receive my diploma for my master's degree at Johns Hopkins University, J. William Fulbright gave an impassioned commencement address that I will never forget.

Mr. Fulbright was the longest serving chairman in the history of the Senate Foreign Relations Committee. One of his accomplishments was the establishment of an international exchange program eventually referred to as the Fulbright Program. The program continues to provide the opportunities for qualifying U.S. citizens to study abroad, and citizens of other countries to study within the U.S. As of 2013, more than 325,400 people have participated in the program since its inception. The purpose of the Fulbright Program was to "bring a little more knowledge, a little more reason, and a little more compassion into world affairs and thereby, increase the chance that nations will learn at last to live in peace and friendship."[17]

Mr. Fulbright centered his speech on the motto of Johns Hopkins University. In Latin, the motto is "Veritas vos liberabit." In English, it translates to "The Truth Will Set You Free." This motto was a slight variant to John 8:32 in the New Testament.

Mikhail Gorbachev

William Fulbright explained why he believed this verse and motto was so true. In 1985, when Mikhail Gorbachev was elected as General Secretary of the Communist Party, his hands were full. The Soviet economy had been stagnant for many years. Mikhail knew it was paramount to revive the Soviet economy. Without a strong economy, the Soviet Union could not survive. He also knew that if the economy was to be successfully turned around, a large number of fundamental changes had to be made.

In 1986, Mikhail introduced glasnost (openness), perestroika (restructuring), demokratizatsiya (democratization), and uskoreniye (acceleration of economic development).[18] During this time, Mikhail turned to and depended on the insights of former Russian Fulbright scholars who had gone to school within the United States. As he was looking for solutions, he wanted to understand what some of the keys were to the U.S.'s economic success. It was the pursuit of truth and real solutions, which began to change Mikhail's mindset and eventually many within the Soviet Union.

Mr. Fulbright emphasized that truth doesn't need to be packaged with a nice bow or contained within a slick sales presentation. In fact, at times slick presentations reek of persuasion and manipulation. He also stressed that too many naively believed it was the strength and fear of the United States that eventually led to perestroika. It wasn't fear that motivated the Soviet Union. It was their desire to find true solutions to their struggles.

Since William Fulbright's speech, we have witnessed what seemed to be impossible. Once people began to taste truth and freedom, they were never the same. Openness wetted the appetite of people in countries throughout Eastern Europe who desperately wanted freedom. For instance, on November 9, 1989, thousands of Germans brought down the Berlin Wall. It led to the end of the cold war.

Fundamental Principles of Democracy

There are important principles we can learn from successful democracies that can help in every aspect of society.

Democratic governments offer the hope that people with different perspectives can enjoy liberties and that they can work together and avoid war. A "Democracy is a form of government in which all eligible citizens are meant to participate equally—either directly or through elected representatives indirectly in the proposal, development, and establishment of the laws by which their society is run."[19]

Sound democracies are based on principles of legal equality and liberty. Legal equality means that all are equal under the law. Liberties are protected freedoms or rights, such as the right to act, speak, and think as one desires without oppression or coercion.

Democracy is not freedom without constraints. There are some who fight against any control. What these people fail to understand is the difference between freedom and liberty. Freedom is the ability to make decisions without external control. Liberty is freedom that has been granted and is protected by a government. John Locke, regarded as one of the most influential of the Enlightenment thinkers wrote, "The end of law is not to abolish or restrain, but to preserve and enlarge freedom. For in all the states of created beings capable of laws, where there is no law, there is no freedom. For liberty is to be free from restraint and violence of others, which cannot be where there is no law."[20]

Liberties Based on Laws of Nature

The U.S. Declaration of Independence states:

> When in the Course of human events, it becomes necessary for one people to dissolve the political bands which have connected them with another, and to assume among the powers of the earth, the separate and equal station to which the **Laws of Nature and of Natures' God entitle them**, a decent respect to the opinions of mankind requires that they should declare the causes which impel them to the separation.
>
> We hold these truths to be self-evident, that **all men are created equal, that they are endowed by their Creator with certain unalienable Rights, that among these are Life, Liberty and the pursuit of Happiness**—That to secure these rights, Governments are instituted among Men, deriving their just powers from the consent of the governed...[21]

The future and success of democracy rests upon virtue and morality. Samuel Adams wrote:

> Neither the wisest constitution, nor the wisest laws will secure the liberty and happiness of a people whose manners are universally corrupt. He therefore is the truest friend to the liberty of his country **who tries most to promote its virtue** and who ... will not suffer a man to be chosen into any

43

office of power and trust **who is not a wise and virtuous man.**[22]

George Washington wrote:

> Of all the dispositions and habits which lead to political prosperity, **religion and morality are indispensable supports**.... And let us with caution indulge the supposition that morality can be maintained without religion.[23]

NEEDS AND OPPORTUNITIES TO CONSIDER

- There will be a growing need for true experts with good diplomatic skills who are truly skilled at offering advice to countries transitioning from authorial regimes to successful democracies.
- With the growth of democracy, we will see a significant increase world-wide in consumer needs for food, clothing, energy, security, employment/contract services, education, health, housing, transportation, investments, consumer goods, hobbies, sports, entertainment, self-improvement, and so on.
- There will be greater competition to provide basic products and services. We will see continued growth in niches and diversification in products and services. Innovation will increase.

INDIVIDUAL EMPOWERMENT

With the spread of democracy, we are seeing the growth of individual empowerment. This is an exciting megatrend. It offers wonderful opportunities for people throughout the world to enjoy basic freedoms and to grow, learn, improve their circumstances, and to have a better life.

Individual empowerment should accelerate substantially during the next 20 years owing to:

- Widespread adoption of communication and technology
- Greater educational attainment
- Poverty reduction and the huge growth of the middle class
- Better health care
- Improvements in manufacturing and technology

With growing freedoms and broader access to improved communications technology, people will be better informed throughout the world. Cost infrastructures once needed to support communications are no longer required. Smart-phones and other communication technologies are enabling people to connect and collaborate.

Education is expanding worldwide. Today, the number of students attending higher education programs is exploding. University enrollment has grown from around 100 million in 2000 to 158 million in 2011. It is expected to reach 263 million by 2025.[24] Education is a key to economic success and will lead to a growth in the middle class throughout the world.

Poverty is being reduced. World Bank President Jim Yong Kim said that "For the first time, the number of people in the middle class surpasses those living in poverty". The NIC believes that by 2030, most people on the globe will be within the middle-class. McKinsey reported in 2010 that the middle class is nearly two billion strong and spends $6.9 trillion annually.[25] Conservative models forecast that 2 billion people will be living in the middle class. Other models estimate that the global middle class will reach 3 billion people by 2030. We will see the most rapid growth in the middle class in Asia, India and Africa.

It is amazing to see how quickly countries are able to grow their GDP per capita. As the graph shows below, it took Britain 155 years to double its GDP per capita. It took the US around 50 years to double its GDP per capita. China and India increased their GDP per capita by over 500 fold in 20 years, but consider also that China and India have about 41 times the population of Britain.

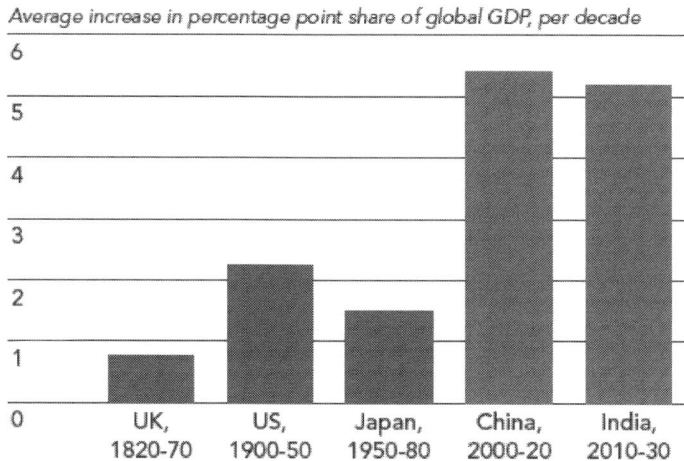

Average increase in percentage point share of global GDP, per decade

UK, 1820-70	US, 1900-50	Japan, 1950-80	China, 2000-20	India, 2010-30

The rapid growth of the middle class has important implications. Demand for consumer goods, including cars, will rise sharply with the growth of the middle class. At the same time, with a shrinking world, we will see accelerated economic competitiveness. This will fuel innovation and specialization.

NEEDS AND OPPORTUNITIES TO CONSIDER

- Collaboration and collaborative technologies will grow in importance. There will be increased desire and need to speak in a common language. The need for better language translation software tools will grow.

- Education will become even more important. Current education structures are expensive and inefficient. Clayton Christensen, who has been given the "number one management thinker in the world award", sees that education is ripe for disruptive innovation. He says we must reevaluate our education systems and rethink our approach to learning. Higher educational costs have risen to unprecedented levels.
- Private universities and even prestigious universities are developing online programs. There will be a growing need for outstanding specialization in education.
- Built-in and just-in-time training will become more vital. There will be a greater need for specialized training for thought leaders and experts.
- The demand for health care services and equipment will grow throughout the world.
- We will see great improvements in manufacturing and technology.

DIFFUSION OF POWER

NIC believes that by 2030, no single country will have a unified, prevailing voice. By 2030, the two largest powers in the world will be China and the United States. Today, the combined economies of the two nations constitute almost 35 percent of the global GDP. Before 2030, China's economy will surpass the United States' economy. While the United States and China will be major international players, they won't possess the same influence that superpowers have held in the past.

By 2030, India could be the new emerging economic giant. NIC believes that Brazil, Colombia, Indonesia, Nigeria, South Africa, and Turkey will also become more prominent players. Brazil will probably be a major player in Latin America and Germany will likely continue to be a leader in Europe.

With the spread of democracy and the growth of individual empowerment, people throughout the world will have improved abilities to influence their governments. People with similar interests and beliefs will naturally come together. Communication technologies will facilitate and enable networks of people with similar interests and beliefs to join together. More networks will have increased influence. Future big internet "moguls" will have an increased ability to predict and influence behavior on a large scale.

NEEDS AND OPPORTUNITIES TO CONSIDER

- There will be a tremendous need for people who have new leadership, collaboration, networking, and motivation skills. Using a strong handed, top down, power approach to getting things done will be ineffective. Pushy motivational approaches will become less effective.
- Collaboration technologies will be in growing demand.

DEMOGRAPHIC PATTERNS

NIC sees four demographic trends that will shape future economic and political conditions:

- Widespread aging
- Shrinking number of youthful countries
- A new age of migration
- The world as urban

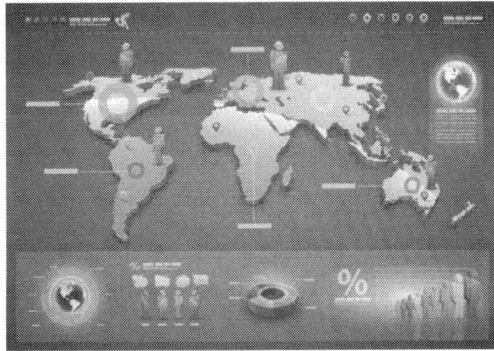

By 2030, the world's population will be around 8.3 billion people; up by 1.1 billion from 2014.

Widespread Aging

People will also live longer. Countries with aging populations (e.g. Japan, Germany, Italy, Greece, Bulgaria, Austria, Sweden, Slovenia, and Latvia) will have slower GDP growths. To fund increased retirement and health care experiences, governments will either have to reduce benefits, increase taxes, reduce government spending, or continue to move toward bankruptcy, leading to economic collapse.

Shrinking Number of Youthful Countries

NIC reports that approximately 80 percent of all armed civil and ethnic conflicts occur in countries with youthful populations. More than 80 countries today have a median age of 25. By 2030, this number will have dropped to 50 countries.

A big reason that countries with youthful populations struggle more with conflict is because it is a challenge for youth in these areas to envision and prepare for a bright future when they can't see economic opportunities on the horizon.

A New Age of Migration

In developing countries, there will be a rapid migration of people into urban areas. Rapid urbanization will lead to a huge growth in construction and transportation.

International migration will increase. Tens of millions of people will likely migrate from poor countries to middle and high-income countries. Developed or emerging countries with aging populations will be eager to recruit young talent. This talent will be more inclined to live in other countries. In an effort to recruit international talent, the need for standard benefit, pension, and social programs will become more apparent.

The World as Urban

In the 1950's, approximately 30% of the world's population lived in urban areas. Today, that number is up to 50 percent. NIC believes that by 2030, 60% of the world's population will live in urban areas.

The UN estimates that from 2011 to 2030, 276 million people in China will move to urban areas. In India, 218 million will migrate to urban areas. Bangladesh, Brazil, Democratic Republic of Congo, Indonesia, Mexico, Nigeria, Pakistan, the Philippines, and the U.S. will continue to see greater urbanization as well.

Urban areas will grow faster than the large city centers. Big cities are already struggling with traffic, infrastructure, health, and sanitation issues. Areas just outside of city centers offer cheaper land. These metropolitan regions will continue to expand and become mega-regions. By 2030, it is estimated that there will be "over 40 large bi-national and tri-national metro regions."[26]

NEEDS AND OPPORTUNITIES TO CONSIDER

- With aging populations, there will be an increased need for businesses that support aging populations (e.g. home-based health care, care centers, dietitians, nutritionists, drivers, fitness, housing, personal assistants, travel guides).
- Governments will also be under pressure to fund larger retirement expenses. There will be increasing pressure to reduce health-care expenses. Innovations to address retirement and health-care will be desperately needed.

- Innovations will be needed to create real economic and educational opportunities for youth—especially in countries with larger youthful populations.
- A real challenge that businesses, communities, and countries have is in successfully creating economic opportunities. Those who are most skilled in successfully helping others to create businesses and develop an economy will be in highest demand. Urbanization creates enormous burdens and is driven typically by economic need vs. a desire to live in a big urban area.
- Innovation, diplomacy, and motivational skills are desperately needed to facilitate improvements in construction, infrastructures, health, and sanitization.

GROWING FOOD, WATER, AND ENERGY NEEDS

With a growing population, expanding middle-class, and urban populations, NIC believes that demands for water, food, and energy will significantly rise. The need for food is expected to increase 35% by 2030. Water demands will increase 40 percent and energy needs will grow 50 percent by 2030. Many countries won't have the capacity to provide these resources and will depend on help from others.[27]

Environmentalists believe that climate change will make these basic resources scarcer. They believe that we will see a decline in precipitation in the Middle East, Northern Africa, Western Central Asia, Southern Europe, Southern Africa, and the U.S. Southwest.

NEEDS AND OPPORTUNITIES TO CONSIDER

- Significant innovations are needed in water management, agriculture, ranching, food processing, and in energy creation and management.

IMPORTANT GAME CHANGERS YOU NEED TO UNDERSTAND

Game-changers are less certain than megatrends, but they are significant variables that could lead to significant changes.

CRISIS-PRONE GLOBAL ECONOMY

The international economy is a crisis-prone economy with much vulnerability. An economic problem in one country can impact the rest of the world.

Even after the 2008 major recession, most developed countries have only begun to reduce their debts. Debt was at the core of the crisis and will take several years and possibly decades before there is economic stability. Debt continues to be a major risk.

Europe and Japan have rapidly aging populations which will likely impact their economies. Aging countries will likely see slow or stagnating growth.

The economies of different countries and regions will move at greatly differing speeds. This will lead to wider economic disparities which introduces risks. The NIC report states:

> The contrasting speeds across different regional economies are exacerbating global imbalances—which was one of the contributing causes of the 2008 crisis, along with straining governments and the international system. The key question is whether the divergences and increased volatility will result in a global breakdown and collapse or whether the development of multiple growth centers will lead to increased resiliency.[28]

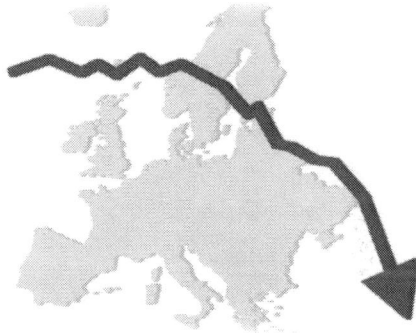

With more countries and regions having a growing voice in world matters, it could become more difficult for national players to cooperate and develop an international economic system that effectively addresses and mitigates economic risks.

U.S. consumer spending played a significant role in the world economy. This will change. Today, over 50% of global economic growth stems from developing countries—especially in Asia and in the South. The world economy will progressively depend on growth in these emerging countries. There will be a strong demand in these emerging countries for infrastructure, housing, consumer goods, and new plants and equipment.

NEEDS AND OPPORTUNITIES TO CONSIDER

- With growing economic disparity, people with expertise and resources will be needed in areas struggling the most, economically speaking, to help create successful businesses and foster successful economic development.
- There will be significant economic opportunities in emerging countries, especially in the areas of infrastructure, housing, consumer goods, new plants, and equipment.
- There will be a growing need for leaders and influencers who can help players with differing perspectives to work together to create and implement a healthy international economic system.
- The inability of governments to manage their budgets is concerning. Overspending creates almost insurmountable problems for this and future generations. The economy is the wherewithal. It is the engine. Political leaders are needed who are willing to do their part to ensure that their governments spend less than what they bring in and use the difference to pay-off debt.
- Consumer spending is also a problem. Consumers need the self-restraint and motivation to live within their means.

THE GOVERNANCE GAP

Communications technology is eliminating the barriers of distance and languages. Communications technology has given people unprecedented ways to collaborate and work together. This has fueled an appetite for democracy around the world.

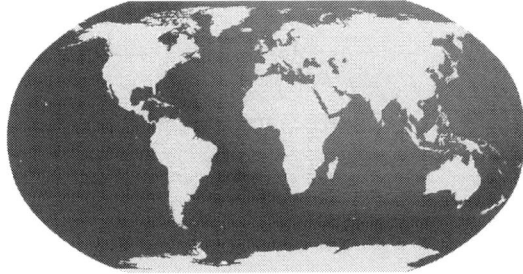

As democracy spreads, more people will want to have a voice in influencing their local and national governments. Worldwide improvements over the last 20 years in communications technology, health, educational levels, manufacturing technologies, and income could continue. There will be a growing demand for governance changes, fair laws, and transparency.

Today, 50 countries are moving from autocratic governments to democracies. These changes are challenging ones and typically take a long time to work out. The transition time can be difficult and dangerous. Changes are usually required in governing structures and practices at all levels.

Countries that are typically most unstable are autocratic and have populations with higher education levels and income (e.g. Gulf, Middle East, and Central Asia countries). The long-term survival of an autocracy depends on its ability to control information and ideas. In the future, that will become more difficult. Also, countries that are democratic, but poor (e.g. Sub-Saharan Africa, Latin America, and the Caribbean, and South Asia) struggle and are also, often unstable.

Today, Western countries have a strong voice in international organizations like the UN Security Council, World Bank, and IMF. This will change. NIC worries that with more players having growing voices in world matters, it will become more challenging for the international community to make decisions and work together to solve major international issues.

NEEDS AND OPPORTUNITIES TO CONSIDER

- Tension and conflict could increase between those who want to enjoy the benefits of autocratic regimes and those who want a greater voice. Transitioning from an autocratic to a democratic government is a difficult one. Experts and thought leaders can assist new leaders in emerging democracies to avoid the risks and implement needed changes.

- Effectively interacting with others, facilitating, influencing, and motivating people with differing viewpoints in a democratic and collaborative manner will be critical skill sets.
- Government organizations throughout the world will need help in successfully becoming more open, transparent, effective, and responsive.

- Countries struggling with poverty will need help in successfully creating new business and job opportunities.
- Communications and collaborative technologies will grow in importance.

POTENTIAL FOR INCREASED CONFLICT

The NIC believes that the risks of interstate conflicts are increasing. The U.S. is less willing to interfere in international affairs. With a growing number of influential players in the world arena, working together to solve international issues could easily be a problem. Getting broad international support is a challenge today. Other world players will be less inclined to support the U.S. as a global protector of democracy. This could lead to greater instability.

There is also a growing risk of small groups or even individuals using destructive tools and weapons (e.g. WMD) that would inflict significant damage. This could spark greater intra- and inter-country conflict.

The NIC report notes that in the last 20 years, there have been fewer armed conflicts and less causality in those conflicts. The likelihood of major powers warring against each other remains low because of the high stakes involved. As countries have grown economically, they have not invested heavily in military capabilities.

NIC believes the risk for regional conflict will be "high during the next two decades in western, central, and eastern portions of Sub-Saharan Africa, in parts of the Middle East and South Asia, and in several Asian-Pacific island hot spots: Timor Leste, Papua New Guinea, the Philippines, and Solomon Islands."[29]

NEEDS AND OPPORTUNITIES TO CONSIDER

- It will be important that political leaders know how to listen, counsel, and collaborate both within and outside of their own countries.
- Listening, counseling, and collaborating with people with differing viewpoints will be an important skill set for everyone to develop.

- Major breakthroughs are needed to stop the proliferation of WMD and other dangerous tools. Additional innovations are needed to detect and protect people from nations, small groups, or individuals who wish to use destructive tools and weapons to inflict damage.

WIDER SCOPE OF REGIONAL INSTABILITY

South Asia and the Middle East are regions where there is the greatest potential for conflict. These are also areas where battles could easily trigger wider conflicts that would have global impact.

South Asia consists of Afghanistan, Bangladesh, Bhutan, India, Maldives, Nepal, Pakistan, and Sri Lanka.

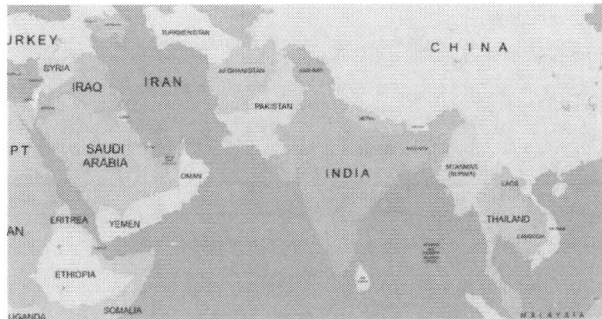

Afghanistan and Pakistan have younger populations and slow-growing economies. "Inequality, lack of infrastructure, and educational deficiencies are key weaknesses in India."[30] The tension between India and Pakistan remains with China backing Pakistan. NIC sees that Asia and the international community are not prepared to effectively mediate and mitigate rising tensions in South Asia.

The Middle East is also a region of major concern. While democracies have emerged in the region, if corruption and unemployment problems persist, people could easily look to hard line Islamic leaders for solutions. The oil producing countries in the Middle East will need to diversify. New technologies will reduce or eliminate the need for oil and gas from the region.

NEEDS AND OPPORTUNITIES TO CONSIDER

- It is vital to world peace that political leaders learn how to listen, counsel, and collaborate both within and outside of their own countries.
- Listening, counseling, and collaborating with people with differing viewpoints will be an important skill set for people generally.
- Oil and gas producing countries in the Middle East need to continue efforts to diversify the products and services they provide.
- Expanding the use of communications technologies will help to broaden opportunities for people to collaborate together.

NEW TECHNOLOGIES

Technology is often a key enabler behind a megatrend or a major change in society. For instance, consider the impact culturally and economically of the printing press, compass, steel, internal combustion engine, telephone, light bulb, electricity, radio, television, penicillin, computers, atomic bomb, nuclear power, and the internet.

There are a number of technologies being developed that could radically change the future. Consider, for instance, how technology is significantly contributing to individual empowerment (e.g. greater education and knowledge, better health care, improved manufacturing).

The NIC believes that the following four technology areas will have the greatest impact on the world:

- Information technology
- Automation and manufacturing technologies
- Resource technologies
- Health technologies

INFORMATION TECHNOLOGY

Big Data

We are moving into the big data period of information technology. Consumers and businesses are moving toward cloud based solutions. New technologies are emerging that help organizations collect, manage, and analyze large volumes of data.

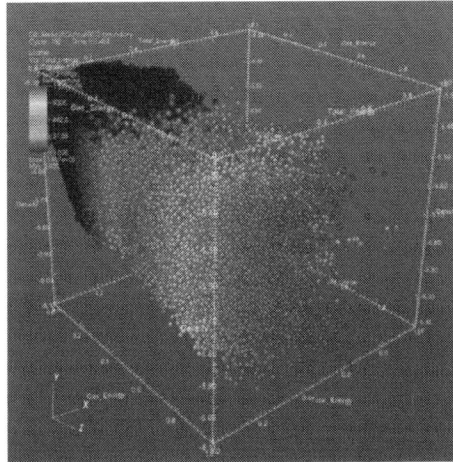

The race is on among businesses to leverage big data to give them a new competitive advantage. Big data can potentially help businesses develop client profiles, see where customers are searching, identify what they are saying online, observe their purchasing behaviors, and determine what they like or don't like about products. It can help businesses develop or refine their products, improve their operations, and increase the effectiveness of their marketing.

Big data and analytics are used for scientific efforts (e.g. weather prediction, physics research, space exploration) and government initiatives. For instance, it is used by law enforcement and intelligence to find criminals and terrorists and ultimately to protect citizens.

Internet companies use data technologies for "web search, targeted advertising, image recognition, language translation, natural language processing, and similar features and functions."[31]

Big data is used for criminal and information warfare purposes. Enemies seek to intercept and disrupt critical communications and information systems that support police, military, air traffic, power grids, banking systems, etc.

Social Networking Technologies

Social networking enables the building of social relations among people who share interests, backgrounds, activities, and so on. Social networks can be used for productive and destructive purposes (e.g. criminal or terrorist agendas).

Social networking technologies are having a far broader impact than imagined possible. They have become important tools for businesses, nonprofit organizations, governments, and informal groups to share information and participate in discussions.

The history of social media is interesting. CompuServe provided dial-up internet service starting in 1969. In 1971, the first email was delivered. In 1978, bulletin board systems were used. Prodigy and America Online began to compete with CompuServe. In 1995, *Newsweek* published an article: "The Internet? eBay! Hype alert: Why cyberspace isn't and will never be nirvana." In 1998, Google enters the scene. In 2001, Wikipedia is started. In 2003, MySpace is launched, and by 2006, it was the most popular social networking site in the U.S. Also in 2006, Twitter was launched.

By 2009, Facebook was the most-used social network worldwide. By 2010, it had over 400 million users and by 2014 it has 1.28 billion active monthly users.

In 2011, social media was used as a vehicle for social change. Social media was used in support of democratic uprisings across the Arab world starting with Tunisia in 2010 and then took hold in Egypt, Libya, Syria, Yemen, Bahrain, Saudi Arabia, and Jordan. Social media was used in a protest movement against social and economic equality that began on September 17, 2001 in New York City's Wall Street area. In 2014, 85% of the world's 7.1 billion people have access to the internet. Around 25% of the world uses social media.[32]

Smart Cities

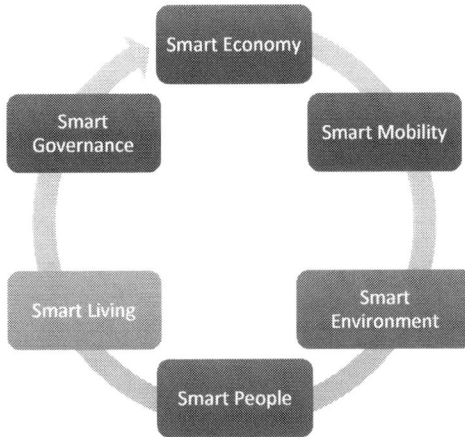

A smart city is defined as "a developed urban area that creates sustainable economic development and high quality of life by excelling in key areas: economy, mobility, environment, people, living, and government."[33]

Integrated solutions provide city officials with a wide array of data that helps them to assess, model, simulate, and plan the city smoother and effectively in many areas (e.g. law enforcement, public safety, transportation, construction, resource management, waste management, environmental controls, communications, security, emergency services, and disaster response).

NIC estimates that "governments around the world could spend as much as $35 trillion in public-works projects in the next two decades."[34] Having solutions to optimize city related decision making and management will become a high priority.

AUTOMATION AND MANUFACTURING TECHNOLOGIES

Automation and advanced manufacturing technologies are fundamentally changing how products and services are designed and manufactured.

Robotics

Robotics, in the past, has been expensive, clunky, and even dangerous. Improvements in robotics are eliminating the need for human labor in certain operations. Advanced robots have improved intelligence, dexterity, and sensing capabilities. These robots are used in a variety of areas (e.g. manufacturing, nuclear, construction, health care, and space and water exploration).

Autonomous Vehicles

Autonomous vehicles can be used on land, sea, or in the air.

Google's self-driving car has made impressive progress. Google has 25 permits to put their self-driving cars on public roads.

Additive Manufacturing

Additive manufacturing, also referred to as 3D printing, is a process of using 3D design data to build up a product in layers by depositing materials.

NIC shares:

> A combination of low-cost machines and online stores of 3D object files could democratize manufacturing and empower individuals, resembling the early days of personal computers and the Internet when small companies were able to make a large impact. Additive manufacturing could lead to large numbers of micro-factories akin to preindustrial revolution craft guilds, but with modern manufacturing capabilities. Such local micro-factories could manufacture significant amounts of products, especially those for which transportation costs are traditionally high or delivery times are long and in the process, shorten and simplify supply chains.[35]

RESOURCE TECHNOLOGIES

Technological breakthroughs pertaining to vital resources will be necessary to meet the food, water, and energy needs of the world's population. Key technologies will likely be at the forefront in this arena and will include genetically modified crops, precision agriculture, water and irrigation techniques, solar energy, advanced bio-based fuels, and enhanced oil and natural gas extraction via fracturing.

Genetically Modified Crops

It is believed that genetically modified crops are key to providing enough food for an expanding population. As of 2010, 10% of the world's croplands were planted using GM crops. Genetically modified crops improve crop yield and reduce the price of food.

There is wide scientific agreement that GM crops pose no greater danger than conventional food. However, some express concerns about the environmental impact and the safety of GM crops. Consequently, there is intense regulatory and public pressure which makes the extensive use of GM plants uncertain. Many consumers and politicians believe there are dangers and inadequate safeguards. So, GM crops face an uphill battle.

Precision Agriculture

Farmers often use the same seeds, water, fertilizers, pesticides, and herbicides and other resources on their fields to grow crops. The problem is the needs of the soil differ widely—even within the same field. To treat a field or fields all the same results in huge waste. Precision agriculture focuses on optimizing the use of resources to get quality crop results and to minimize negative environmental impact.

Water Management

Farming today consumes approximately 70 percent of the freshwater that is available today. Current irrigation methods waste 60 percent of the freshwater. The cost of water run through desalination technologies is too expensive to use for farming. Improved micro-irrigation systems can help, but they are expensive. Precision agriculture, genetically modified crops, and hydroponic greenhouse technologies can help as well.

Bio-Based Energy

Bioenergy is renewable energy from biological sources. In other words, it is energy that comes from naturally replenished biological resources. These resources include agriculture (e.g. straw), forestry (e.g. wood), and biological-derived waste (e.g. manure). "The Global 2030" Report states that:

> As bio-based energy becomes cost competitive, it could enable advanced biofuels and other products that derive from nonfood sources to at least partially replace current food-crop-derived biofuels and petroleum feed stocks in the next 15-20 years.

> ...A transition to bio-based energy produced from nonfood biomass would radically alter world energy markets and be essential to improving food security.[36]

Solar Energy

Solar energy comes from using the sun to generate heat or electricity. Solar energy is in abundance and it generates vast amounts of energy.

Photovoltaic technology is now widely used for electrical power generation. Solar thermal technology can also generate electrical power by using mirrors to concentrate sunlight, which is converted to heat in a solar collector. However, whether solar-photovoltaic or solar-thermal electricity-generating plants will be cost competitive with other electricity-generating fuel sources— coal, natural gas, nuclear, or wind— is unclear. Some forecasts indicate that the projected costs of electricity production from natural gas and coal will remain lower than electricity production from solar power in the next 15 to 20 years.

HEALTH TECHNOLOGIES

New health technologies will continue to extend the average age of populations around the world, improve debilitating physical and mental conditions, and improve overall well-being.

Disease Management

Without using diagnostic and detection tests, it can be difficult and even impossible for physicians to determine what illness a patient has. Getting test results can take time and, in some cases, the delays are life threatening. Quick, effective, and inexpensive diagnostic and detection devices are key to disease management.

New disease management technologies (e.g. molecular diagnostic devices, theranostics, and synthetic biology) will expand the length of life and improve the quality of life. Improvements in disease management technologies could be expensive and could be out of reach for people who do not have health coverage.

Human Augmentation

Human augmentation generally refers to technologies that improve human productivity or capability or helps to overcome physical or mental limitations of the body. Human augmentation technologies include implants, prosthetics, and exoskeletons.

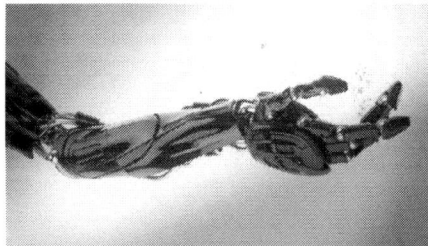

Implants are man-made devices (vs. transplants), often made of biomedical material (e.g. titanium, silicone, apatite). Examples of implants include pins, rods, screws, plates, artificial pacemakers, cochlear implants, and drug-eluting stents. Prosthetic limbs today can provide equivalent or slightly improved functionality to human limbs. Brain-machine interfaces in the form of brain-implants are demonstrating that directly bridging the gap between brain and machine is possible. The military is using exoskeletons that allow personnel to carry increased loads.

ADDITIONAL HIGH IMPACT EVOLVING TECHNOLOGIES

Knowledge Automation

Over the last decade, there has been a debate as to what percentage of the workforce was knowledge workers. In a *Business Week* article, Evan Rosen argued that every worker today is a knowledge worker.[37]

Today, artificial intelligence systems are making it possible to automate knowledge work. Computers can answer complex spoken questions. IBM Watson is a great example. When Watson is asked a question, it identifies the hypothesis, evaluates the evidence from different data sources, and then provides responses based on probabilities. Watson can be applied to almost any body of knowledge. For instance, IBM Watson is focused on the medical profession. It helps doctors make diagnoses and select treatments. "Watson can ingest more data in a day than any human could in a lifetime. It can read all of the world's medical journals in less time than it takes a physician to drink a cup of coffee. All at once, it can peruse patient histories, keep an eye on the latest drug trials, stay apprised of the potency of new therapies, and hew closely to state-of-the-art guidelines that help doctors choose the best treatments. Watson never goes on vacation and it never forgets a fact. On the contrary, it keeps learning."[38]

Knowledge automation systems open the world to major workforce changes over time. Some knowledge work can be completely automated. Knowledge tools can be used to assist highly complex jobs.

Digital Biology

As the analog world of biology is put into the digital world and this information is analyzed over time with artificial intelligence and machine language systems, we will begin to see more clearly how genes, diseases,

DNA, the brain, and protein folding works. With the insights gained, researchers will be able to predict and improve an individual's future health.

Next-Generation Genomics

McKinsey identified next-generation genomics as a top disruptive technology. Genomics is a brand of molecular biology focused on the function, structure, and mapping of genomes. A genome contains an organism's complete set of DNA. It took 13 years and $2.7 billion to sequence a human genome. Today, a human genome can be sequenced in a few hours and for a few thousand dollars. Instead of using a trial and error method of testing, scientists can thoroughly test how genetic variations can lead to specific traits and diseases. The next focus is to customize organisms by "writing" DNA. Breakthroughs here would have a significant impact in medicine, agriculture, and in other areas.[39]

Advanced Materials

Researchers are discovering how to create smart or designed materials that have properties that can be changed in a controlled fashion by external stimuli (e.g. electric or magnetic fields, light moisture, pH, pressure, stress, temperature).

Researchers have discovered how to create smart materials, memory metals, and nanomaterials. Nanomaterials could significantly impact the economy. "At nanoscale (less than 100 nanometers), ordinary substances take on new properties—greater reactivity, unusual electrical properties, enormous strength per unit of weight—that can enable new types of medicine, super-slick coatings, stronger composites, and other improvements. Pharmaceutical companies are already progressing in research to use nanoparticles for targeted drug treatments for diseases such as cancer."[40]

NEEDS AND OPPORTUNITIES TO CONSIDER

- Technology is becoming a key enabler in almost every field and discipline. Developing a sound understanding of technology will most certainly prove to be valuable.
- The need for technology and engineering experts will grow rapidly. Technology offers great promise if it is developed to help mankind in noble pursuits.

- Advancements in social networking technologies can help people to connect and collaborate to develop new innovations.
- Smart city technology offers the hope that cities of the future will be designed well and optimized.
- Robotics will help to increase quality and productivity.
- Autonomous vehicles can help save lives and provide us additional time.
- Additive manufacturing technologies (e.g. 3D printing) could lead to exciting new breakthroughs in manufacturing and supply chains.
- Genetically modified crops, precision agriculture, and water management can help provide the food and water resources that the world needs.
- Bio-based, solar, battery, and other energy breakthroughs can help to mitigate pollution problems, conserve natural resources, improve energy output, and decrease costs.
- Health technologies can save lives, improve the quality of life, and human capacity.

THE ROLE OF THE UNITED STATES

From 1865 to 1918, over 27 million Europeans immigrated to the United States. By the late 1800's, the U.S. became the world's leading industrial power.

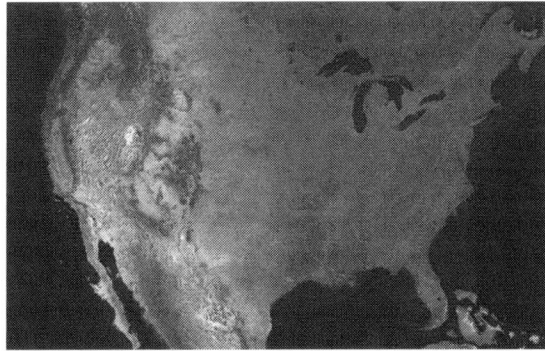

After the American Revolution, the U.S. won a long series of wars from 1785 to 1919. The United States entered World War I in 1917, and joined the Allied Forces to bring about a successful and decisive victory in 1918, ending the German, Russian, Ottoman, and Austro-Hungarian empires. After the bombing of Pearl Harbor on December 7, 1941 the United States entered World War II. By August of 1945, the Third Reich collapsed, Vichy France was dissolved, and the Japanese and Italian empires were defeated. Following World War II, the United Kingdom started to lose its influence and the United States and the Soviet Union began to be regarded as the two superpowers that dominated world affairs.

Today, the U.S. is confronted with a number of internal challenges. Health care costs are considerably higher (50% higher than other developed countries) within the U.S. than in other developed countries. The U.S.'s secondary education is poor. The median household income has been declining in the U.S. since 1999. Less money as a percent of income is being spent on military spending and more money is being spent for entitlement programs. This trend will likely continue with rapidly growing Social Security, Medicare, and Medicaid costs.

As of 2013, the U.S. is still the most inventive country. It holds 27.9 percent of all international patent applications. The U.S. has 44 percent of the top universities in the world. The U.S. also has rich natural resources.

The NIC report suggests that:

> Continued prosperity in emerging market countries where approximately one billion people will be added to the world

middle class by 2030 could play to U.S. economic strengths. These newly empowered consumers will demand education, entertainment, and products and services driven by information technology— all goods the U.S. excels in producing. Moreover, as a global technology leader, the U.S. economy could be motored by innovations in medicine, biotechnology, communications, transportation, or energy.[41]

NIC believes that by 2030, the U.S. will still remain "first among equals" among world players. It will still be the leading military power in 2030, but its relative military strength will be weaker. Its economy will still be the largest at market exchange rates. China's economy will be the largest in terms of purchasing power.

There are considerable risks for the world if the U.S. cannot solve its challenges. The U.S. has played an important role in focusing the attention of the world on terrorism, proliferation of destructive weapons, and in addressing regional conflicts that could impact international order. Without the U.S. continuing to play a key role, there will likely be increased security risks worldwide.

The big question is what role will the U.S. have in the future and what will be the impact of a world where there are more players at the decision-making tables (e.g. UN, IMF, and World Bank) with their own interests and agendas in mind?

NEEDS AND OPPORTUNITIES TO CONSIDER

- U.S. political leaders are needed who can move past the finger pointing blame game and roll up their sleeves and simply work to address vital issues that impact both the U.S. and the world. They must eliminate the government debt and deficit spending. Multi-year plans to curb deficit spending ultimately leading to a balanced budget haven't worked and lead to delays. These leaders still need to address health care costs. They are 50% higher than in other developed countries.

  Additionally, they need to improve the secondary educational system so their students have increased capabilities to contribute.

- Effective international leaders and innovators are needed to work together to develop effective solutions for fighting terrorism and stopping or controlling proliferation of destructive weapons.
- It will be vital to world peace that future political leaders know how to listen, counsel, and collaborate both within and outside of their own countries to effectively address problems.
- There will be increased needs in education, entertainment, and products and services driven by information technology.

4. KEYS TO BUSINESS SUCCESS—MOVING FORWARD

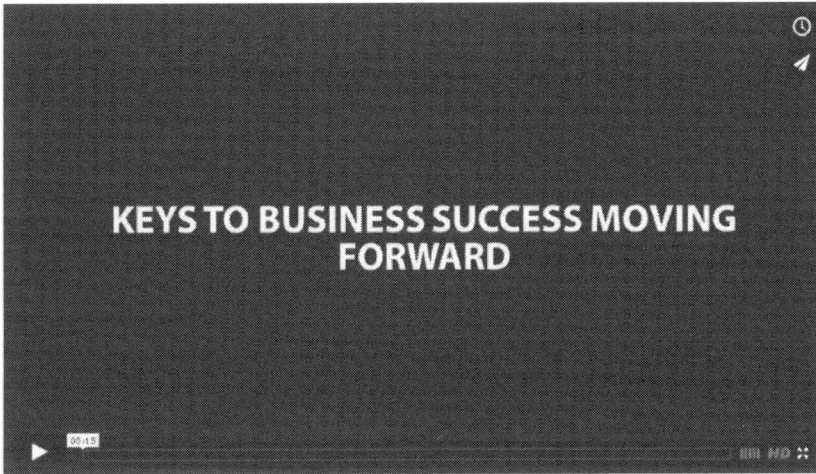

KEYS TO BUSINESS SUCCESS MOVING FORWARD

http://creating-you-inc.com/book-videos/

One of the most heart-breaking experiences people have is putting their heart into a business and then see it fail. It is also stressful working for a business that is struggling. Understanding the keys to business is vital to your career success.

There are countless theories, books, research studies, case studies, courses, workshops, and seminars on this topic. How do you really find out what works?

Tony Robbins accurately said that, "Success Leaves Clues." Often, the answers are right in front of us, but the question is, can we find them in all the noise and clutter?

What we have done in this chapter is to identify the most important factors that lead to success. We have done that for:

- **The Most Admired Companies in the World**
- **The Most Profitable and Admired Companies in the World**
- **The Businesses that Warren Buffet (the Wealthiest Investor) Invests In**

We also share and highlight findings from the "**Digital Reinvention**" report produced by IBM based on inputs they received from 1,100 C-Suite executives. The report predicts a new and different economy that is exciting and merits serious consideration.

In the section "Changing Competitive Playbooks", we review the underlying assumptions of competitive playbook models that have been at the foundation of the most successful businesses for several decades.

NEEDS AND CHANGING MARKETS

Virtually all industries and businesses are focused ultimately on people. Somehow in the over compartmentalization and segmentation of industries, markets, functions, and skill sets, most employees have lost a clear and accurate understanding of the needs of those they ultimately serve. This is why some of the most successful companies today started off in a garage less than twenty years ago. With fewer traditional competitive barriers (learn more in "Changing Competitive Playbooks), we will see a dramatic increase in new, unheard of small companies today becoming the innovators of tomorrow.

Returning to the Needs of People

As we become more hyper-connected, innovative/product oriented, and team focused, there will be a rapid race to truly put the customer back on the center stage. To survive, there will be less rhetoric and hype and more of an intense focus on customer needs.

As humans, we all have the same basic needs and desires. If we understand the basic nature of people, their greatest needs and wants, and their patterns of decisions and actions, we will have a better chance of succeeding.

Below, you see a diagram that synthesizes insights from two helpful models of human needs: Abraham Maslow's "Hierarchy of Needs," and Choe Madanes' "Human Needs."

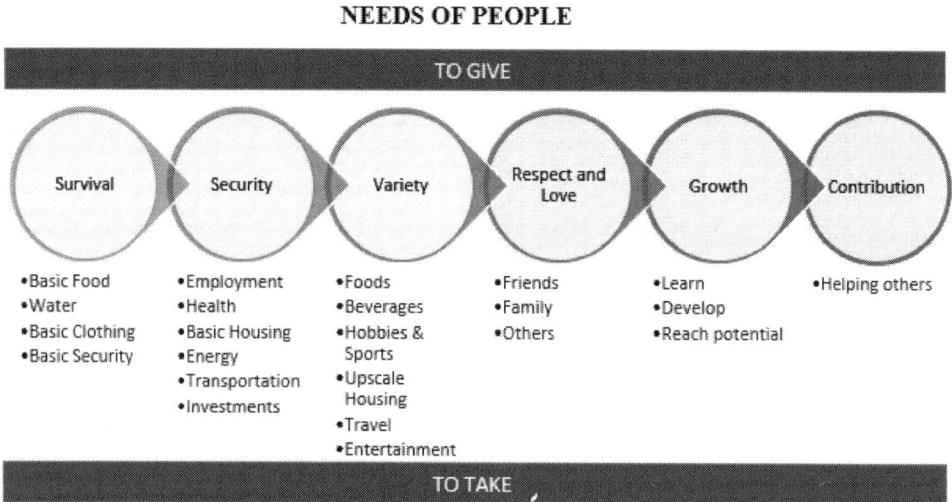

NEEDS OF PEOPLE

TO GIVE

Survival	Security	Variety	Respect and Love	Growth	Contribution
•Basic Food	•Employment	•Foods	•Friends	•Learn	•Helping others
•Water	•Health	•Beverages	•Family	•Develop	
•Basic Clothing	•Basic Housing	•Hobbies & Sports	•Others	•Reach potential	
•Basic Security	•Energy	•Upscale Housing			
	•Transportation	•Travel			
	•Investments	•Entertainment			

TO TAKE

How Industries Align with People's Needs

It is important to return to the core purpose of business. By simplifying and putting the customer center-stage, we can ignore the unnecessary complexities of segmentation (e.g. industries, functions) and look for innovation opportunities. On the next page, you see examples of industries that align with those needs. Almost all industries and businesses align.

SURVIVAL	SECURITY	VARIETY	RESPECT & LOVE	GROWTH	CONTRIBUTION
Agriculture	Appliances	Beverages	Communications	Education	Charities
Electric	Auto	Broadcasting	Electronics	Experiences	Churches
Oil and Gas	Computers	Dairy	Entertainment	Publishing	Nonprofits
Meat	Construction	Electronics	Food		Publishing
Security - Policy	Construction	Entertainment	Hobbies		
Security - Military	Drug	Food	Music		
Textile	Education	Hobbies	Publishing		
Water	Financial	Housewares	Photographic		
	Health	Housing	Sporting Goods		
	Health Insurance	Leisure Travel			
	Health Services	Lodging			
	Hospitals	Meats			
	Long-Term Care	Music			
	Medical	Personal Products			
	Office Supplies	Photographic			
	Oil and Gas	Publishing			
	Shipping	Recreational			
	Staffing	Sporting			
	Technology	Textile			
	Transportation	Toys			

Discovering Disruption Opportunities

For decades, market researchers have focused on identifying attributes of consumers—relating to demographics, personality, behaviors, values, interests, etc. Researches searched and found correlations between attributes and purchasing behaviors.

Clayton Christensen, the seminal author of disruptive innovation books like *The Innovator's Dilemma*, believes that focusing on customers by attributes is an indirect and less effective way to develop and sell products and services. He says that the direct way to determine what a customer's needs are is to look at the jobs that they need to accomplish. He explains that our days revolve around things that we need or want to do or accomplish. He emphasizes that a key way to gather insights is to look at the outcomes or jobs that people are trying to accomplish and determine better ways to help them accomplish their desired outcome.

Major industry, market, business, product, and service innovations can be developed by focusing on the outcome that a consumer or business needs or desires, then move on to developing a breakthrough to meet the need, then eliminate or reinvent the means to providing the outcome.

Look at Amazon.com. Formerly, books were sold primarily in bookstores. Amazon invested heavily on selling books over the internet. Today, they are the top online retailer and the 16th overall largest retailer in the world. Google, eBay, Netflix, Pandora, and PayPal are other examples of market innovators.

Finding Disruptive Innovation Opportunities

The key to finding disruptive innovation opportunities is as simple as starting with the customer and their needs. In the left column of the table on the next page, you see examples of needs. In the second column, you see a high-level description of the current approach to addressing the need. In the last column, you see a new approach to meeting these needs. There are leading-edge technologies being used for some of the new approaches below—but they are not widely deployed.

Needs	Current Approach	New Approach
Food	Determine what to eat. Purchase ingredients or pre-prepared foods. Prepare foods as needed. Put out plates, utensils and food. Clean and put away extra food, pots, pans, plates, utensils, etc.	Determine what to eat. Smart kitchen prepares food, cleans and puts everything away.
Water	Water is piped in from water system.	Use home water generating equipment.
Clothing and Shoes	Shop, try on, and purchase desired clothing.	Choose desired fashion from computer. 3D clothing printer prints clothing and shoes.
Basic Security	Call police if there is an issue. Police may arrive, investigate, and process the issue. Consumers hope for a good outcome.	Smart surveillance systems built into home, vehicle, and other devices. Potential issues are detected and information is automatically recorded, analyzed by police databases, and processed for prompt action.
Employment	Receive education, training, and experience. Look for a job, apply, interview, check references, conduct background, get hired, and travel to and from work.	Receive basic education and use quick job or project work search tools. References and background checks are automated. Work from home using powerful collaboration software. Receive just-in-time training while working (e.g. knowledge automation, help resources, training modules). Paid for results. Get automatic certifications and degrees based on work, demonstrated knowledge, and outcomes.
Health	Go to doctors, dentist or other health specialist for a physical symptom or for check-up.	Health sensors and apps provide ongoing information about your health. Information is tied to knowledge information systems (e.g. IBM Watson). You schedule a video consultation with a medical professional to review your data. The data from sensors or

		medical exams automatically links into early health issue detection systems.
Housing	New home construction: Develop architecture drawings, find contractor, have home built over 4-6 months with traditional building supplies, put in landscaping.	Go online and easily create design of a highly customized home. Modularized components are compiled or built with smart materials using additive manufacturing system in 3-5 days by local contractor. Home assembled and landscaping completed in 3-5 days.
Transportation	Get in vehicle, get fuel, oil and other fluids as needed, and drive on roads with stop signs, yellow lights, red lights and busy roadways. Arrive at your final destination.	Get in friction-free, low-weight, low-cost, minimal parts, self-driving vehicle. Traditional roads are no longer needed. The driving system provides transportation and energy to all vehicles.
Investments	Research countless investment options with an advisor or by yourself. Invest your savings and retirement depending on your risk tolerance, on what your advisor recommends or you believe is the best investment options.	Invest in equity-based crowd funding projects that you are involved with. These are projects that best align with your passions, talents, and strengths. Work on projects is highly transparent to all investors.
Leisure Travel	Spend time researching options to find the ideal travel options based on budget. Plan out details. Travel is somewhat stressful because of the coordination that is required.	Travel is safe, relaxing, inexpensive, and non-intrusive to nature. Traveling accommodations are spacious and as comfortable as staying in 1-2 rooms within your own home.

WHAT INSIGHTS DOES THIS PROVIDE YOU THAT YOU COULD USE?

As you look at many of the most admired companies (e.g. Apple, Amazon, Google), you see that many of these firms built their products and/or business models on disruptive innovation opportunities.

- What niche ideas do you have at this point?
- What disruptive innovation opportunities are there that you could tap into?
- Are there innovation products or services you could develop?
- Is there a new business model you could adopt?

MOST ADMIRED COMPANIES

There are nine key factors or enablers that are at the foundation of the success of the top twenty most admired companies. They include:

1. **New Trends**: Businesses identified, understood, and built upon trends not fully tapped into by others.
2. **Innovation**: Company introduced new or significantly improved products, services, business models, or marketing approaches.
3. **Technology:** Firm leveraged existing and/or created new technologies.
4. **Marketing**: Business effectively marketed their business, product, and service.
5. **New Business Model**: Company created a new way to develop and deliver value to customers.
6. **User Design**: Firm provided a great experience for the users of their products.
7. **Customer Experience**: Business created a pleasant overall experience for customers as they learned about, purchased, received, and used the product or service.
8. **Patents and Other Rights**: Company secured patents, trademarks, or other rights.
9. **Cost:** Firm became the lowest cost provider.

Key Enablers by Company

Below, you see the top twenty most admired companies along with the key enablers they tapped into to succeed:

1. **Apple**: Innovation, Technology, Patents, User Design, New Trends, Marketing, New Business Model.
2. **Amazon.com**: Innovation, Technology, New Trends, New Business Model, Costs.
3. **Google**: New Trends, Innovation, Technology, Patents, New Business Model.
4. **Berkshire Hathaway**: Investments. See "The Businesses that Warren Buffet Invests In."
5. **Starbucks**: Quality, Customer Experience.
6. **Coca-Cola:** Marketing, User Design, Quality.
7. **Walt Disney**: Innovation, Customer Experience, New Trend.
8. **FedEx**: New Business Model, Innovation.
9. **Southwest Airlines**: New Business Model, Costs.
10. **General Electric**: New Trends, Innovation, Technology.
11. **American Express**: Customer Experience.
12. **Costco Wholesale**: Costs, New Business Model.
13. **Nike**: Marketing, User Design.
14. **BMW**: User Design, Innovation, Technology.
15. **Procter & Gamble**: New Trends, Innovation, Patents, Marketing.
16. **IBM**: New Trends, Innovation, Technology, Patents, Marketing.
17. **Nordstrom**: Customer Service, Quality.
18. **Singapore Airlines**: Customer Service.
19. **Johnson & Jonson**: New Trends, Innovation, Patents, Marketing.
20. **Whole Foods Market**: New Trends, Customer Experience.

WHAT INSIGHTS DOES THIS PROVIDE YOU THAT YOU COULD USE?

Make it a priority to develop your knowledge and skills and/or business in several of these areas below:

- **New Trends**: Accurately identifying and knowing how to tap into new trends.

- **Innovation**: Developing innovative products and services that are successful.
- **Technology:** Fully leveraging and developing new technology.
- **Marketing**: Successful marketing in the new world.
- **New Business Model**: Developing new business models.
- **User Design**: Understanding best practices in user design.
- **Customer Experience**: How to develop outstanding customer experiences.

MOST PROFITABLE BUSINESSES

The most profitable businesses tap into five additional enablers to try and secure their long-term economic success.

1. **Capital Investment**: Significant capital or fixed assets investments.

2. **Economies of Scale**: Developing a cost advantage due to high quantities produced and lower per-unit fixed costs.
3. **Political Influence**: Lobbying and gaining support of influential political players.
4. **State Supported**: Backed, once owned, or currently owned by a nation.
5. **Mergers and Acquisitions**: Purchasing and/or joining with other companies.
6. **Investments**: Making investments in business acquisitions and/or the stock market

List of Top Ten Most Profitable Businesses in the World

As of October 21, 2014, the most profitable businesses are[42]:

1. **Industrial & Commercial Bank of China**: State Owned.
2. **Apple:** Innovation, Technology, User Design, New Trends, Marketing, New Business Model.
3. **Gazprom**: State Backed.
4. **China Construction Bank**: Was State Owned
5. **Exxon Mobil**: Capital Investment, Economies of Scale, Political Influence.
6. **Samsung Electronics**: Innovation, User Design, Technology, Operations, Marketing, Political Influence.
7. **Agricultural Bank of China**: Was State Owned.
8. **Bank of China**: State Owned.
9. **BP plc:** Capital Investment, Economies of Scale, Political Influence.
10. **Microsoft**: Innovation, Technology, New Trends.

WHAT INSIGHTS DOES THIS PROVIDE YOU THAT YOU COULD USE?

Some of the most profitable businesses are truly innovators and provide exceptional value to consumers. Others are state supported. There are few truly innovative state supported businesses. As global economy expands and innovations grow, state supported businesses will find it more difficult to change and compete.

Some of the most profitable businesses are oil companies. The oil industry is ripe for disruption. Oil companies still believe that few vehicle drivers will see electric cars in their lifetime. They believe that electric cars will comprise only 4 to 5 percent of total cars in the market over the next 20—30 years.[43]

Banking, finance, insurance, and related businesses are ripe for major disruptions. Max Levchin, a co-founder of PayPal, said "the reason I get up in the morning is because I fundamentally see an opportunity to remake finance."[44]

THE BUSINESSES THAT WARREN BUFFETT INVESTS IN

Another approach to determine which companies are most successful is to look to top investors and see what they invest in. Warren Buffett is the wealthiest and most successful investor in the world. So, what does he look for before he invests? In simplest terms, he looks at the:

- Longevity of a company, the per-share (earnings / total shares) progress of a company
- If the stock is selling at a 25% or more discount to its real value

His great skill is in determining the real or intrinsic value of a stock or business. Value is determined based on both tangible and intangible factors. The intangible factors are what complicates things. When assessing the value of a stock or company, it is believed that Warren looks at past earnings, estimates growth rates, identifies his confidence margin, and then compares the rates with a financial product he has 100% confidence in (e.g., Treasury bond).

It appears that as of June 2014, Berkshire Hathaway's top stock investments were in the following companies:

1. **Wells Fargo**: Capital Investment, Mergers and Acquisitions, Political Influence
2. **Coca Cola Co.**: Marketing, User Design, Quality
3. **American Express**: Customer Service
4. **IBM**: New Trends, Innovation, Technology, Patents, Marketing
5. **Wal-Mart Stores**: Cost, New Business Model
6. **Procter & Gamble**: New Trends, Innovation, Patents, Marketing
7. **Exxon Mobil Corp.**: Capital Investment, Economies of Scale, Political Influence
8. **U.S. Bancorp**: Capital Investment, Mergers and Acquisitions, Political Influence

Warren Buffett has said that they are going to focus more on buying complete operating companies rather than just stock positions.

WHAT INSIGHTS DOES THIS PROVIDE YOU THAT YOU COULD USE?

Warren Buffett's investment strategy is largely focused on businesses that have a sustained competitive advantage. How a company develops a competitive advantage will matter more in the future. IBM and Procter & Gamble are two companies that are great innovators and provide significant value to their customers. Too many firms gain a competitive advantage simply by creating barriers to entry in an industry. Too often, this strategic approach leads to a company putting themselves first above the interest of the customers, health, environment, or other critical factors.

THE "EVERYONE-TO-EVERYONE" ECONOMY

The IBM Global Business Services Division believes that the digital technologies will lead to drastic changes in the economy. They interviewed 1,100 C-Suite executives on the future impact of digital technologies. Of the 1,100 executives:

- 58% said social, mobile, analytics, and cloud will reduce barriers to entry
- 69% believe that these new technologies will increase competition
- 41% expect that competition will come from outside

In the Digital Reinvention report titled "**Digital Reinvention**" prepared by Saul Berman, Anthony Marshall, and Nadia Leonelli, they describe how the economy will change. They explain that there are three different economies at play: 1. the organization-centered economy, 2. the individual-centered economy, and 3. the "everyone-to-everyone" economy.[45]

Organization-Centered Economy

The organization-centered economy was most prominent during the early part of the 20th century. This economy was driven and dominated by producer-driven consumption. Ford and its Model T is an example. They designed, manufactured, and sold standardized cars.

"Organization-centered economies are comprised of industries characterized by high barriers to entry and capital-intense production with larger enterprises controlling product."[46]

Individual-Centered Economy

Today, we are in the individual-centered economy. In other words, individual needs and wants are driving the economy. Companies today are developing differentiated products based on different customers. Additionally, they are focused on providing customers a seamless experience across channels. Furthermore, they are beginning to tap into analytics from their big data sources to help drive their products and operations.

Everyone-to-Everyone-Centered Economy

The "everyone-to-everyone" economy is "characterized by hyper-connectedness and collaboration of consumers and organizations across the gamut of value chain activities: co-design, co-creation, co-production, co-marketing, co-distribution and co-funding. In this integrated system, consumers and organizations work together to create value with transparency driving trust and effectiveness. The implication for value creation and allocation will be profound. Kiva.org, the microfinance non-profit site, is an example."[47]

WHAT INSIGHTS DOES THIS PROVIDE YOU THAT YOU COULD USE?

Consider now how to become a leader in the "everyone-to-everyone" economy. As it makes sense, determine how and where you can connect and collaborate with customers around the products you have in mind. Consider how you might connect and collaborate with others in the value chain to design, produce, and distribute.

CHANGING COMPETITIVE PLAYBOOKS

There are competitive playbooks based on old proven practices that businesses around the world use as a foundation to build their products and services around.

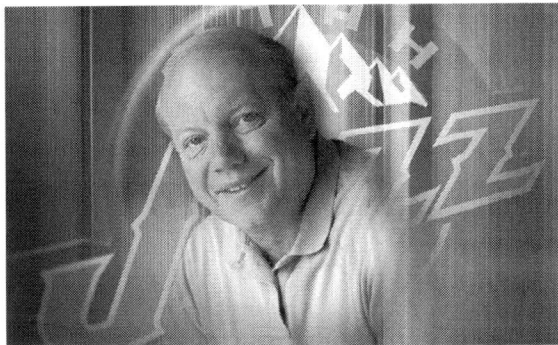

As I worked for Larry H. Miller, the owner of the Utah Jazz NBA basketball team, the Salt Lake City Bees minor league baseball team, and numerous other businesses, we would often refer to sport analogies as we discussed business. Larry and his son Greg would share how vital it was to master the basics. That is one reason why Larry was such a powerful and successful entrepreneur and businessman. The basics became so ingrained that they became second nature, instinctive, and leveraged in a fraction of a second without thinking.

Serious coaches and players study their game. They look carefully at what offensive and defensive plays lead to what results. They focus on their own strengths and weaknesses. They determine what plays best align with strengths they have. The coaches and players focus on mastering the plays and developing the strengths needed to execute the plays well. Having the best playbook, the best strengths, and continuously building upon the strengths you have is needed to excel.

Businesses and products fail at the most rudimentary level. Often, they are not performing the basics needed to begin playing in the game and the statistics verify this. Between 80 to 90% of new businesses fail. Approximately 80% of new products fail to meet expectations. Around 70% of projects fail. The reasons they fail is because typically, they have not: collected customer input, differentiated themselves in the market, and have not communicated their value in a clear, concise, and compelling manner to the right audiences.

Peter Drucker said, "**Business is about marketing and innovation. Anything beyond this is a cost.**" So, your goal should be to become the best innovator and marketer you can within a niche. The key to finding the right niche is to identify and focus on your noble passions and your natural talents. You can best discover the best playbook for yourself and turn your talents into valuable strengths by seeking to become a:

1. **True thought leader in your niche**
2. **Master of innovation within your niche**
3. **True expert in effectively communicating with your target audience**

OLD PLAYBOOK BASICS

You need to understand the old playbooks that have helped businesses to succeed for many years. These playbooks are used extensively today. Some of the rules are changing which we will review later. However, you can't leverage the reasons for the changes without understanding the old plays.

FOUR GENERIC STRATEGIES

Michael Porter from Harvard Business School is one of the most respected strategists in the world. Among his many works, he identified three generic strategies that companies in any industry could adopt to successfully compete. We have modified his generic strategies to simplify the language and to include a fourth—relating to marketing. Frequently, multiple companies can sell the exact same product and one will excel while the others struggle—simply because of effective marketing.

For many years, successful businesses focused on one or more of the following four approaches to develop a competitive advantage:

- Creating a **different and/or better product**
- Become the **low cost** provider for a product
- Focus on a **niche segment** of a market that large companies overlooked
- More effectively **market** their company and product

If you concentrated on developing **different and/or better products,** you would invest in R&D, secure patents, and other intellectual property rights, purchase special equipment, and develop a variety of products that the competitors weren't offering.

If your focus was on **low costs**, you would reduce supplier, manufacturing, distribution, and/or processing costs.

If you employed a **niche segment** approach, you would offer customized products and/or outstanding customer service to a niche segment of the market.

If a key to your competitive advantage was **marketing**, you would excel at branding and positioning in an effort to motivate consumers to be loyal to your products and services.

SO, WHAT IS CHANGING?

Creating a Different and/or Better Product

This generic strategy is becoming increasingly more important and is progressively becoming the lifeblood of the economy.

Innovation is becoming more vital. Competition to innovate and create different and better products is accelerating. Product life cycles are continuing to shrink.

In the future, companies will invest more in design, modeling, simulation, testing, market research, knowledge, and new manufacturing systems.

Become the Low Cost Provider for a Product

We are seeing major disruptive changes in this area. As automation, robotics, additive manufacturing, remote access, and other technology improves, the need for centralized manufacturing and outsourcing will become less important. For instance, future additive manufacturing (e.g., 3-D printing) technologies will be able to manufacture automobiles, food, shoes, furniture, lighting, homes, human organs, and so on.

Focus on a Niche Segment of a Market that Large Companies Overlooked

The trend toward niche products and services will continue to grow rapidly. Technology will enable manufacturers or consumers to quickly customize products to meet specific customer needs.

More Effectively Market their Company and Product

Today, positioning and branding is highly effective, but also, incredibly risky and expensive. Improvements are being made in the online world to better target and market to specific audience segments.

FIVE FORCES FRAMEWORK

Michael Porter identified five forces that shape every industry. His five forces framework has been integral to business strategies of top firms around the world. To sustain a competitive edge, you needed to successfully prevail in one or more of the five forces.

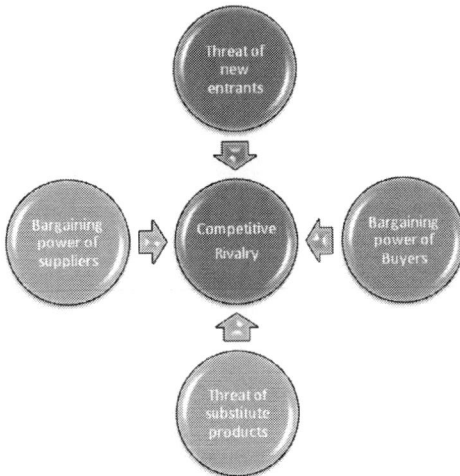

Threat of New Entrants

The objective here is to dissuade new players from entering the market. Efforts to deter new players include: high capital requirements, economies of scale, unique distribution channels, political pull, patents, positioning, branding, marketing, customer loyalty, product differentiation, and alternatives.

What is changing?

- High capital investment costs will continue to be a deterrent. However, people will look for alternative ways to; for instance, utilize expensive capital equipment. Approaches will include co-creation, shared purchase or rental use of equipment, discovering cheaper substitutes to accomplish the same task, or developing one's own equipment at a lower cost.
- Economies of scale will progressively become less of a deterrent as we increasingly move toward a "produce-on-demand" business model.
- Political pull will become less important as constituents have greater access to information and more influence.
- Acquiring and enforcing patents will become more challenging in a global economy where innovation is accelerating and product life cycles are decreasing.
- As we move more toward customized products and services, niche positioning, branding, and direct response marketing will become more important. Broad-brushed marketing will be less effective.
- Product differentiation will be vital and offering product alternatives will be expected.

Threat of Substitute Products or Services

The goal here is to offensively or defensively introduce or protect yourself against substitute products or services. Roku, Hulu and Netflix are examples of technologies that are replacing cable and satellite TV.

What is changing?

- The threat of substitute products or services will continue to be a real threat.

Bargaining Power of Customers

The objective here is to reduce the bargaining power of customers. Bargaining power is the ability of customers to apply pressure on a firm. For instance, if enough customers have product or service alternatives, their bargaining power is high. Firms seek to become the only provider of a high-demand product or service that others cannot compete against.

What is changing?

- Competing on price will become more difficult. Consumers today are offered more alternative products and services. Developing the capacity to address the growing and dynamic needs of customers will be key to success. Innovation, design, excitement, high value, and quality will grow in importance.

Bargaining Power of Suppliers

When there are more suppliers competing in the same marketplace, the bargaining power of each supplier diminishes. As a supplier, your ideal goal is to get exclusive rights to sell high-demand, profitable products. Also, you seek to establish strong distribution channels.

What is changing?

- As the world moves more toward a local "produce-on-demand" model, the future will progressively become more difficult for suppliers who are only the middle-men. Those who have local facilities to both manufacture and sell products will likely do well.

Competitive Rivalry

A high degree of competitiveness within an industry deters new entrants. Mature markets often compete on price with lower profit margins. Competition is continuing to grow at a rapid rate with the growing global economy. Keys to success are to innovate, protect your innovations, provide product alternatives, establish a powerful brand, thereby making it expensive for others to advertise, establish powerful distribution channels, and so on.

What is changing?

- Important keys to success were: innovation, patents, establishing a powerful brand, and building powerful distribution and sales channels.

Keys to success in the future are innovation, customized products, and services, local "produce-on-demand" manufacturing, and effective targeted, direct response marketing and brand awareness.

WHAT INSIGHTS DOES THIS PROVIDE YOU THAT YOU COULD USE?

High capital investments, economies of scale, and patents may over time, become less important. The key to your success is to become a thought leader in your area. Become connected with others who have expertise in other portions of the value chain needed to conceive, design, develop, market, fund, and manufacture.

5. What Careers Will Be in High Demand?

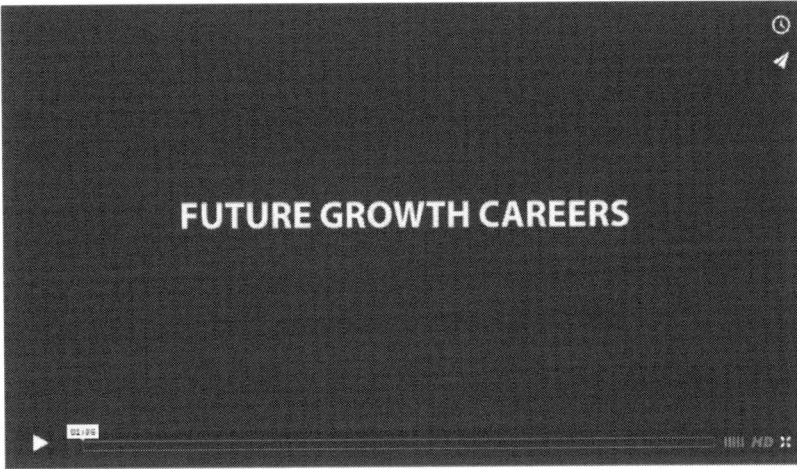

http://creating-you-inc.com/book-videos/

In this chapter, we identify the:

- Most Important Knowledge and Strengths Needed Across Fields
- Fastest Growing Occupations of $100,000 or Higher
- Ten Fastest Growing Industry Sectors
- Largest Industries

We will also identify careers and businesses that relate to vital roles (e.g. peacemakers, problem-solvers, opportunity-makers, health and care givers, protectors, innovators) needed in the world.

MOST IMPORTANT KNOWLEDGE AND STRENGTHS NEEDED ACROSS FIELDS

As subject-matter expertise, innovation, and technology become the backbone of future success, having the knowledge and skill sets below will become important across all fields or niches.

1. **Vision**: The ability to see real needs and solutions and inspire others to work with you to work toward a compelling vision of the future
2. **Strategic Foresight**: The capacity to identify and understand relevant trends. Being able to collect, interpret, and predict outcomes based on data and information; the skill of accurately forecasting outcomes and developing effective strategies and plans
3. **Problem-Solving:** The skill to accurately understand root causes and develop solutions that successfully address problems
4. **Innovation**: The capacity to create new or significantly improved products and services
5. **Thought Leadership:** The skill to become an authority in your specialization or niche; committed to the field and to a better future
6. **Technology:** The skill of understanding relevant technologies, seeing how to leverage them, see where they are going, and how to use or develop new technologies
7. **Marketing:** The ability to understand current and future target customers and their needs; the skill of communicating in a way that helps people to learn about you or your organization and to want to purchase from you

BUREAU OF LABOR STATISTICS PROJECTIONS

The Bureau of Labor Statistics (BLS) projects what occupations and industries will be in the greatest demand in the future. Their labor force projections are developed based on careful analysis. They consider and factor in:

BUREAU OF LABOR STATISTICS
U.S. DEPARTMENT OF LABOR

- the future size and composition of the population
- economic models
- consumption and investment projections
- industry output estimates
- occupational job projections
- education and training needs.

The BLS reviews their projections regularly to determine where and why there were variances and they identify what can be done to improve accuracy and publish the results.

We will review the following labor projections provided by The Bureau of Labor Statistics (BLS):

- Highest Paying Occupations
- Fastest Growing Occupations of $100,000 or Higher
- Ten Fastest Growing Industry Sectors.

HIGHEST PAYING OCCUPATIONS

According to the BLS, the top 20 highest paying occupations between 2012 and 2022 will be as follows:

1. Anesthesiologists, Internists, Obstetricians & Gynecologists, Orthodontists, Surgeons
2. Psychiatrists
3. Family and general practitioners
4. Prosthodontists
5. Chief executives
6. Dentists, specialty
7. Pediatricians, general
8. Dentists, general
9. Nurse Anesthetists
10. Petroleum engineers
11. Architectural and engineering managers
12. Air traffic controllers
13. Computer and information systems managers
14. Marketing managers
15. Pharmacists
16. Podiatrists
17. Judges, magistrate judges, and magistrates
18. Natural sciences managers
19. Airline pilots, copilots, and flight engineers
20. Lawyers[48]

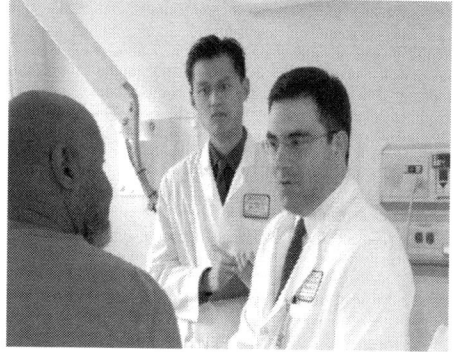

FASTEST GROWING OCCUPATIONS OF $100,000 OR HIGHER

According to the BLS, the fast growing occupations with an average median income of $100,000 or higher are:

1. Petroleum engineers
2. Nurse anesthetist
3. Anesthesiologists
4. Surgeons
5. Mathematicians
6. Podiatrists
7. Political scientists
8. Physicians and surgeons, all other
9. Physicians and surgeons
10. Orthodontists
11. Dentists, general
12. Psychiatrists
13. Oral and maxillofacial surgeons
14. Dentists
15. Pediatricians, general
16. Computer and information systems managers
17. Computer and information research scientists
18. Prosthodontists
19. Family and general practitioners
20. Pharmacists[49]

TEN FASTEST GROWING INDUSTRY SECTORS

The ten fastest growing industry sectors, according to the BLS from 2012 to 2022, are expected to be:

1. Home health care services
2. Individual and family services
3. Outpatient, laboratory, and other ambulatory care services
4. Management, scientific, and technical consulting services
5. Computer systems design and related services
6. Cement and concrete product manufacturing
7. Office administrative services
8. Offices of health practitioners
9. Veneer, plywood, and engineered wood product manufacturing
10. Facilities support services[50]

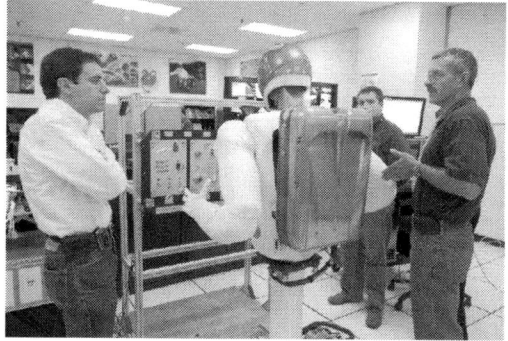

LARGEST INDUSTRIES

Understanding what the largest industries are today helps you to understand where the biggest needs are that people spend money on. According to Fidelity, today's largest industries according to market capitalization are as listed below:

1. Oil, Gas, & Consumable Fuels
2. Banks
3. Pharmaceuticals
4. Diversified Telecommunication Services
5. Insurance
6. Software
7. Internet Software & Services
8. Media
9. Technology Hardware, Storage & Peripherals
10. Real Estate Investment Trusts
11. Capital Markets
12. Beverages
13. IT Services
14. Food products
15. Chemicals
16. Semiconductors & Semiconductor Equipment
17. Biotechnology
18. Metals & Mining
19. Food & Staples Retailing
20. Automobiles

PEACEMAKERS

Peacemakers help to address emotional struggles and conflict. The need for peacemakers is growing rapidly.

Depression rates are increasing. The Centers for Disease Control and Prevention reports that depression affects 9.1% of adults in 45 states, DC, Puerto Rico, and the U.S Virgin Islands.[51] And, approximately 6.7% of adults meet the requirement for **major** depression.[52] Moreover, the number of patients diagnosed with depression is increasing approximately 20% each year.

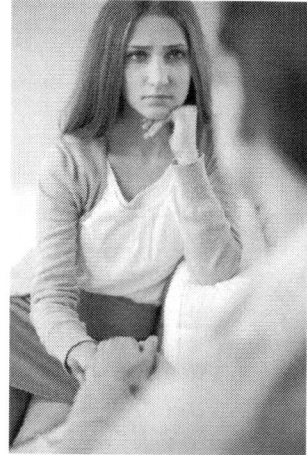

Divorce rates are increasing. The sexual revolution from 1950 until 1980 led to half of all marriages in the U.S. ending up in divorce. Two economists had once claimed that in the 1980's, divorce rates began to decline. However, demographers from the University of Minnesota later found that divorce rates didn't decline, but rather they flattened. They also found that the age-standardized divorce rate has increased by 40% since 1980.[53]

The world is becoming a smaller place. With the growth of democracy and individual rights, more people will want to become connected and share their voice. With the diffusion of power, more countries will want a voice in world affairs. Old "command and control" leadership styles will no longer be effective in governing.

Peacemakers help people, organizations, communities, and countries to diplomatically address their concerns. Individuals, at times are in a state of turmoil and need help. Organizations often have tension between employees, among managers and employees, and between different departments. Communities and countries have people with different and strong voices.

The world is in desperate need of peacemakers. Peacemakers successfully help others to adopt wholesome values of kindness, love, and dedication to others.

Effective peacemakers:

- Cherish pure values
- Understand emotional needs and issues
- Possess deep and real love for others
- Seek to fully understand the full truth
- Teach by example as well as in word
- Can see and understand the real intentions of people
- Are objective and don't have an agenda
- Are perfectly honest and without guile
- Constantly focus on the good of others
- Are in control of their emotions
- Possess a quiet confidence in themselves
- Are persuasive
- Are patient
- Are direct when needed

Examples of peacemaker careers:

- Facilitators
- Arbitrators
- Diplomats
- Psychologists
- Counselors
- Social Workers
- Clergy
- Human Resources
- Politicians
- Consultants
- Customer Service Representatives
- Child Care
- Teachers

PROBLEM-SOLVERS

Countries and communities are confronted with major security, economic, criminal, social, political, and environmental issues. People are confronted with economic, physical, mental, and spiritual issues. True problem-solvers are needed more than ever.

Problem-solvers never throw up their hands and say the problem can never be resolved or "I can't make a difference." True problem-solvers find hope, look for the light at the end of the tunnel, and continually seek to resolve problems.

Examples of problem-solving careers:

- Scientists
- Engineers
- Software Engineers
- Professors and Teachers
- Medical Doctors / Dentists
- Strategists and Organization Builders
- Military Leaders

You don't always have to focus on the macro-problems to make a real difference. Your actions can make a world of difference in the lives of a few people. Your example can have an even greater impact. Mother Teresa is a perfect example. A journalist heard of her efforts to rescue the destitute in Calcutta. The reporter told Mother Teresa that, "statistically speaking, she was accomplishing absolutely nothing." She responded that her work was about love and not statistics. She said she could keep the commandment to love God and her neighbor by serving those within her reach with whatever resources she had. "What we do is nothing, but a drop in the ocean," she would say on another occasion. "But, if we didn't do it, the ocean would be one drop less [than it is]."[54] Mother Teresa set an example for millions by serving one person at a time.

OPPORTUNITY-MAKERS

Opportunity-makers help to create changes for others to contribute and become self-reliant. They help others to improve economically, mentally, spiritually, and physically.

Business and economic development is needed throughout the world. Education is a key enabler that helps to create opportunities for others— but it is not sufficient. When young people have limited employment opportunities, they are more inclined to turn to crime or conflict as a means to provide or gain the respect of their peers.

Examples of opportunity-maker careers:

- Economic Developers
- Social Entrepreneurs
- Nonprofit Leaders
- Entrepreneurs
- Business Leaders
- Economists
- Political Leaders
- Professors/Teachers
- Engineers
- Strategists

HEALTH AND CARE-GIVERS

The demand for health professionals and care givers will continue to grow throughout the world as more people have the economic means to pay for medical help, and as people live to be older and populations age.

Personal care and home health aides are within the top four of the fastest growing occupations. Home health care services and individual & family services are the two fastest two growing industry sectors.

Nine of the twenty highest paying occupations are medically related. Sixteen of the twenty fastest growing occupations paying $100,000 or higher are within the health field.

Examples of heath and care-giver careers:

- Medical
- Nursing
- Obstetrics
- Dentistry
- Personal and Home Care

PROTECTORS

Protectors help to ensure that others can enjoy the right to life, liberty, and the pursuit of happiness. Protectors are those who are willing to sacrifice all that they have to protect not only the people they love, but those that they don't.

Examples of protector careers:

- Law Enforcement
- Military & Defense
- Intelligence
- Security

INNOVATORS

Innovators can be problem-solvers and opportunity-makers as well as peacemakers. In a growing, competitive, global economy, innovation will be the key to success. Those careers and skills needed to successfully innovate and create compelling new products and services will be in high demand.

Examples of innovator careers:

- Market Researchers
- Engineers
- Product Managers
- Software Developers
- Medical Scientists
- Architects

Science, technology, engineering, and mathematic related skills will also become increasingly important.

6. HOW TO BECOME A THOUGHT LEADER IN YOUR NICHE

Thought leaders are the foremost authorities in a specialization or niche. They are committed to their field and to a better future. Thought leaders often bring people together to share insights and grow.

As the economy moves more toward specialization and innovation, expert knowledge will become more critical. In a crowded and competitive marketplace, the appetite to tap into the insights of thought leaders will grow.

Your passion for your field will grow as you see how it can benefit others. As you make time to continually learn and eagerly look for answers, develop and test new ideas, share insights and bring people together, your contribution to the field will grow. As you continue to do these things, you will naturally become a thought leader. You won't need to declare yourself as a thought leader. Your peers will do that for you.

Here are questions to think about to help you become a thought leader:

- Where and how can you get access to the best thinking and learning in your niche?
- How can you continuously test and apply the new knowledge you gain to solve problems?
- How can you develop new insights that lead to breakthrough results?

But, I'm Not an Expert Yet

You may be telling yourself, "but, I'm not an expert yet". Until you become an expert, there are things you can do to both make money and develop your expertise.

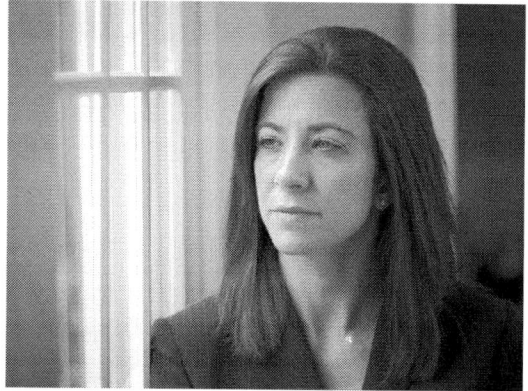

- **Focus on beginners in the niche:** We typically lose our ability to communicate in layman's terms to beginners as we become more of an expert. Often, those best able to help people just getting started are those who just recently and successfully learned themselves.
- **Become the interviewer**: You can find the thought leaders, interview them, and create products and services around the knowledge you gather.
- **Become the researcher**: You can research the niche market, gather insightful data and information, and convert those insights into valuable products.
- **Become the bundler**: You can take your product and bundle it together with other valuable products that you have re-sell rights to.

Begin Now to Grow Your Network

You want to begin soon to develop your network so that you can connect and learn from others, discover needs, and share valuable insights. Here are tips to help you develop a successful network:

1. **Review your target audience and determine where they meet; offline and online.**

   Research where your target audience meets offline. Is it through associations, conferences, lectures, etc.? Identify where they meet online. Is it in LinkedIn groups, Facebook groups, membership sites, or forums?

2. **Join and contribute to associations, groups, and other networking groups.**

   The temptation for most people is to focus their networking exclusively on people who have the exact same interests or vocations as they do. For example, let's say you are a strategy consultant. You might join the Association for Strategic Planning, the Strategy Management Society, and various LinkedIn strategy groups. Many members of these groups are strategy consultants like you. While helpful, it is important to find groups that your target audience is a part of. For example, if you are focused on strategy consulting in the automotive industry, you may want to join groups with automotive executives.

3. **Identify and study the top offline and online influencers in your niche.**

   To find out who the top influencers are in your niche, do searches, review top publications, and ask others in your groups. See who the best book sellers are in your niche. Use various online tools to find who has the most online influence (e.g., Buzzsumo.com, Klout.com, PeerIndex.com, Kred.com, Hashtagify.me).

4. **Systematically grow and engage with your social media network.**

   Find and follow people who are part of your target audience. Promote outstanding posts, articles, and videos that provide helpful insight. Share your knowledge in a way that best helps others to succeed.

7. MARKET RESEARCH TO FIND OPPORTUNITIES

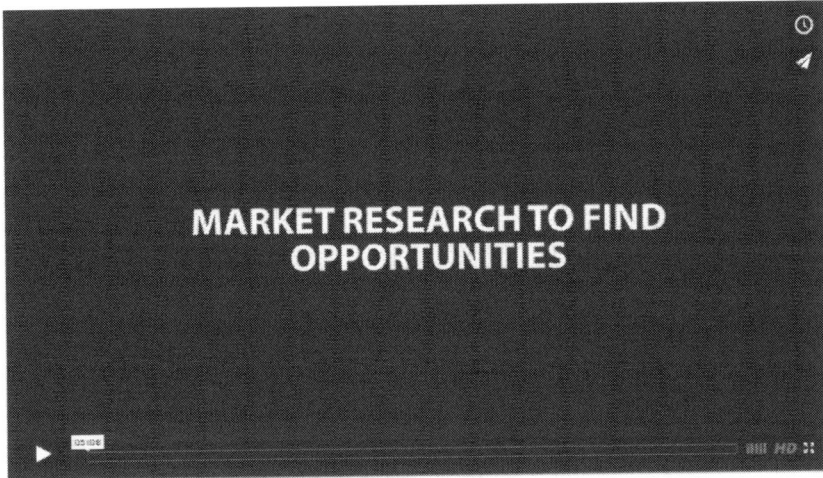

http://creating-you-inc.com/book-videos/

Developing products and services helps you to understand more clearly the needs of your target market. It focuses you on assisting to resolve their pains or achieve their aspirations. It helps to develop you into an expert and a thought leader. It can be the key to your business.

There are a wide variety of products and/or services that you can provide relating to your field. They include:

- Books
- Webinars
- Online courses
- Membership sites
- Live workshops
- Seminars
- Individual coaching
- Group coaching
- Consulting
- Mastermind groups
- Speaking
- Software
- Reports

THE MARKET RESEARCH AND PRODUCT DEVELOPMENT PROCESS

The following is a simplified product development process you can use. There are more complex models; but often, the essence of what is important gets lost in unnecessary complexity.

Initial Market Research → Target Customer → Detailed Market Research → Requirements → Iterations & Feedback → Marketing

INITIAL MARKET RESEARCH

The first step to developing a winning product is to conduct market research. As you conduct market research, your objectives are to:

1. Identify similar products and services that are successful
2. Understand why they are successful
3. Collect customer input
4. Develop initial product requirements to build a superior product

We will show you simple, but powerful sources of information you can tap into to help you begin steps 1 through 3.

Asking the Right Questions

In the book *A More Beautiful Question: The Power of Inquiry to Spark Breakthrough Ideas*, Warren Berger says that the most creative, successful people in the world tend to be expert questioners.[55] There are important market research questions that you need to ask and strive to get answered before you begin developing your offerings. You need to be objective and avoid trying to convince yourself that there is a market for something when there isn't. Below are examples of basic questions you need to focus on:

Demand

- Is there enough demand in your target niche?

Pain/Urgency/Passion

- Are your target customers confronted with pain and a sense of urgency to find a solution?
- Are they motivated by a strong passion?

Searching

- Are your target customers actively searching for a solution to their problem?

Competition

- Are there limited options today for your target customers?
- What are the best products and services in the niche?
- Why are they the best?
- What marketing approaches do they use?

Why the Best?

- Where do the top providers come up short?
- Should you focus on a narrower niche?
- How could you focus on a narrower niche and provide a solution that better meets needs?

Frustrations

- Where do the top performing products and services come up short?
- Are these shortcomings easy or difficult to solve by the competition?

Profitability

- What is the average selling price for similar products or services?
- Could this be profitable for you (profits minus costs)?

Places to Research

Before you start your research, develop a system you are comfortable with to capture and examine your findings. It is too easy to jump into a search mode and forget that you need a way to retrieve and analyze your results.

Where you should research will depend on the type of product you want to develop. For instance, if you want to publish a book, Amazon.com offers rich information. You can identify best sellers by category. For Kindle books, you can locate the Amazon best seller rank number and plug that number into a tool like KDP Calculator. KDP Calculator provides you with an estimate of how many units of the book are being sold on a daily basis.

The internet can provide you rich data. Over 70% of all purchase decisions are made after doing an internet search. For products like online courses, membership sites, live workshops, seminars, coaching, consulting, mastermind groups, software, and reports—web analytics are especially helpful. There are four web analytic tools that offer free services that are incredibly valuable in helping you in your research.

- **Google Keyword Planner**: This helps you discover the volume of search traffic for keywords, learn how much competition there is for keyword traffic, and it suggests bid prices for the keywords. The higher the bid price, the more competition there is for the keywords. More competition suggests there is higher demand. That means there are paying customers. You can review ads and learn who is providing what products, and how they are marketing their products.
- **Market Samurai**: Provides research tools to help you find ideal keywords to use, analyzes the 10 top-ranked competitors for target keywords, finds domain names you could use, and helps to discover monetization opportunities.
- **SEMRush**: Gives you access to search engine results from 106 million keywords and 71 million domains. The data includes search volume, competitor's keywords, ad strategies and budgets, backlinks that competitors have, and much more.
- **Buzzsumo.com**: Steve Rayon reports that 1% of content marketing articles receive 30% of all shares. Buzzsumo.com enables you to see which topics, by content type, get the most attention in social media channels and who the top influencers are. It helps you find content that

resonates with your audience, conduct competitor research, and to create or curate and share popular content.

Affiliate networks (e.g., Clickbank.com) are another place where you can see what is selling and what isn't. Within Clickbank.com, you can visit the marketplace, pick a category, and then sort results by the following filters:

- **Initial $ per sale**: How much commission you make per offer
- **Average % per sale**: Commission rate the product owner offers
- **Average Rebill**: Recurring revenue the affiliate receives
- **Popularity**: Overall sales quality of the product
- **Gravity**: Tells you the number of different affiliates who have made a sale in the last 60 days. Products with gravity over 30 are selling well.

Once you find top selling products related to your target niche, you can click on sales pages of the products being sold to learn more about the product and how they are marketing it.

YOUR TARGET CUSTOMER

"The aim of marketing is to know and understand the customer so well the product or service fits him and sells itself."—Peter Drucker[56]

Most marketers look at the customer from only one or two vantage points. The goal should be to develop a 360 degree understanding.

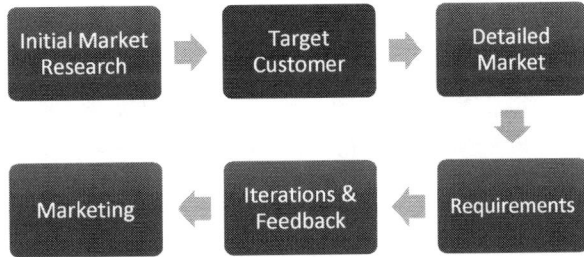

The clearer you can become about your target customers, the better you will be able to create a superior product that best meets their needs.

One of the most useful tools to help you focus on is a customer profile. There are four steps to defining your target customer profile:

1. Identify the basic demographics of your target customer
2. Review the human needs model and refine the profile
3. Look at market segmentation approaches to refine the profile
4. Begin your interviews with target customers and finalize your profile

Identify the Basic Demographics of Your Target Customer

This could include location, gender, age, income, occupation, education, household size, and the stage of the target customer in their family life cycle (e.g., newly married, married with teenage children, empty nesters.)

Please see the example below.

Review the Human Needs Model and Refine Your Target Customer Profile

The better you can understand the full breadth of needs that your target customer has, the more you can understand where they are coming from and how to best serve them.

Looking at basic human needs models can offer powerful insights. Ravi Sawney, one of the top product designers in the world, along with co-author Deepa Prahalad, published the New York Times best-seller book *Predictable Magic.* It discusses how to use Maslow's Hierarchy of Needs model to develop winning products.

The next model is a combination of Maslow's *Hierarchy of Needs* and Choe Madanes' *Human Needs.*

NEEDS OF PEOPLE

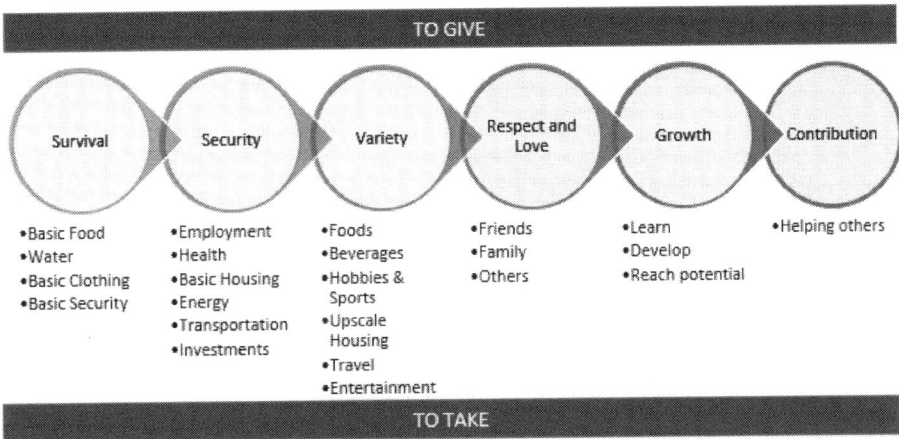

TO GIVE

Survival	Security	Variety	Respect and Love	Growth	Contribution
•Basic Food •Water •Basic Clothing •Basic Security	•Employment •Health •Basic Housing •Energy •Transportation •Investments	•Foods •Beverages •Hobbies & Sports •Upscale Housing •Travel •Entertainment	•Friends •Family •Others	•Learn •Develop •Reach potential	•Helping others

TO TAKE

Look at Market Segmentation Approaches to Refine Your Target Customer Profile

The key here is to ask the right questions. There are several approaches that are used to segment a market so that you can determine what their wants and needs are. The traditional segmentation approaches include:

- Geographic
- Demographic
- Socioeconomic
- Psychographic
- Behavior
- Culture
- Benefits

Job-to-be-done: Clayton Christensen suggested that focusing on customers by their attributes is both an indirect and ineffective way to develop products. A more useful and direct way to determine what a customer's needs are, is to look at the jobs that they need to accomplish. His approach is referred to as the "job-to-be-done" approach.

Noble passions: Many products today are designed around appealing to peoples' baser and selfish passions. Focus instead on helping to bring out the best in people. What are their good or noble passions and how can you help them succeed?

127

Talents and strengths: Another angle is to look at people from the perspective of talent and strength. What are their talents and strengths and how can you help them build upon those.

Below is an example of a more comprehensive customer profile.

CUSTOMER PROFILE SUMMARY

Basic Information
- Geographical: Philippines
- Gender: Male or Female
- Age Range: 24 - 40
- Income: Low income
- Occupation: Professional
- Education: Bachelors or higher in technology field
- Household Size: 2+
- Newly married or young kids

Safety and Security
- Worried about providing stable income for immediate and extended family in current location
- Concerned about heath of family members

Physiological
- Many of the technology jobs are lower end jobs, and are in congested cities – away from friends and family
- Feel big uncertainty about finding a job with good growth opportunities

Fears, Pains, Frustrations
- Very worried that will need to move to Manila away from friends and family. Worried that will be stuck in lower-end technology job and hate job

Hopes and Desires
- Dream is to be able to start an international technology business and provide technology jobs in home town

James Cruz

Personality, Activities, Interests, Lifestyle, Values
- Personality: People person, innovative, visual & hands-on learner.
- Activities: Involved in economic development and youth development activities
- Interests: Passion for technology, business management, international relations & soccer. Active volunteer in civic and church organizations
- Lifestyle: He is an "aspirer" and "explorer"
- Values: He has strong religious Christian values

Behavioral
- Desired benefits: Would love to get training, mentoring and even partnering with someone who could help him to achieve his goals
- Loyalty: Very loyal
- Customer Status: Potential customer – but doesn't have much money

Job-To-Be-Done
- Wants to have the knowledge, tools, mentoring to develop a successful international technology consulting business

Product-Related
- Would love the "in-person" but currently can afford "hybrid" version of program

DETAILED MARKET RESEARCH

Review Best Products

Superior products have five times the success rate, over four times the market share, and four times the profitability of "me too," copycat, reactive, and ho-hum products, with few differentiated characteristics.[57]

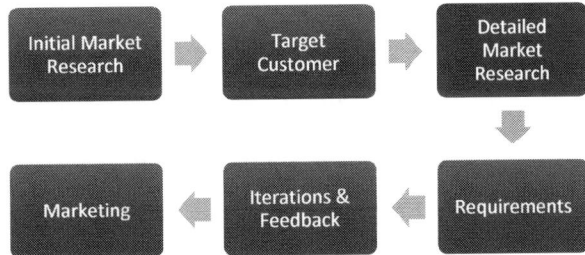

To develop a superior product, you need to understand competitive products. It can also pay to look at the best products outside of your niche, field, or industry.

Develop a list of detailed questions to help in your reviews. Below are examples of generic questions to help you get started,

- Who is their target customer?
- What problem, aspiration, or job are they focused on helping the customer with?
- What customer benefits do they offer?
- How successfully do they meet the most important needs of the customer?
- What features do they offer?
- Where are their gaps?
- How do they market their product?
- Are they the first provider of products in the niche?
- How are they unique from the others?
- In what way could you be the first and most unique in your niche?

Gather Target Customer Input

There are different ways to gather customer input. One-on-one interviews, customer site visits, camping out with the customer, customer panels and usability labs are some of the best approaches. What can be especially helpful is to set up a process to gather iterative customer inputs as you develop mock-ups and ultimately, your product.

To motivate target customers to participate, you could offer them your product free or at a discount. If they aren't interested, then it could be that you are:

- focused on the wrong target customers
- not communicating the value effectively
- not showcasing your product in a way that is seen as being valuable enough for them to want to participate at this point

One-On-One Interviews

One of the simplest ways to get started and to gather valuable insights is to simply ask people that fit within your target audience. You can start by conducting simple interviews that take as little as 15 to 30 minutes. Below are examples of simple questions you can ask initially:

- What are your greatest pains, worries, and obstacles?
- What are your greatest hopes and aspirations?
- How do you try to accomplish the task today and what would be ideal?

Make it a point to record the words (especially the emotional words) that they use. This will help you both in designing your products and your marketing campaigns.

Customer Site Visits

Sometimes, customer site visits where you can talk with customers within their environment can be insightful. When you conduct a customer site visit, have a clear purpose in mind. Develop questions and/or a plan of what you want to observe.

During a customer site visit, ask open-ended questions. If you ask questions, identify their struggles and problems. Learn what task or job they are trying to accomplish. Find out what their pains or frustrations are. Discover their goals and plans. Whatever you do, don't make the mistake of talking about your product and how it can help them.

Observing Customers

Customers often say one thing and do something different. Observing what customers actually do offers rich insights.

Customer Panels

Customer panels are groups of consumers who have agreed to provide ongoing input. Panels can respond to questions, offer inputs on mock-ups, prototypes, and iterations of a product. A significant benefit of customer panels is that they can provide you quick input.

Usability Labs

A usability lab is where usability tests are conducted. For instance, an interviewer can ask a person to perform certain tasks. Observers watch to see how the person carries out the task.

8. How to Develop Your Compelling Products and Services

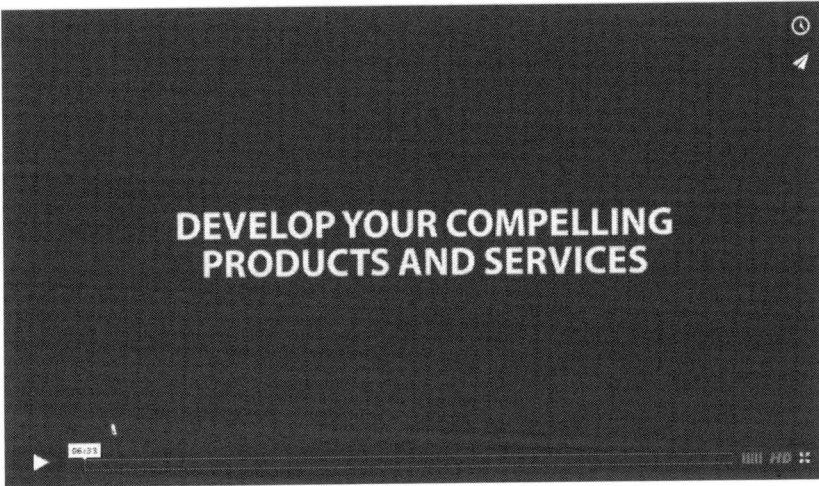

http://creating-you-inc.com/book-videos/

What are the Keys to Developing a Winning Product?

According to Gartner, approximately 80% of new products fail. Over 70% of projects and strategies fail as well. Key reasons for failure include:

- A superior product was not developed
- The voice of the customer was not built into the product
- Little or no market and customer research was conducted
- An effective launch and marketing plan was not developed and implemented

Dr. Robert G. Cooper is one of the most influential innovation and product development thought leaders in the world. He was named the "World's Top Innovation Management Scholar" by the U.S. Journal of Product Innovation Management. He spent 40 years studying the practices and pitfalls of 3,000 new products in thousands of companies. From his experiences, Dr. Cooper provided insights on how to succeed in product development. On the following page are some highlights from his findings.

A. Striving for Unique Superior Products

Delivering products with unique benefits and real value to customers separates winners from losers more often than any other single factor. Such superior products have five times the success rate, over four times the market share, and four times the profitability of "me too," copycat, reactive, and ho-hum products, with few differentiated characteristics.

There are similarities among superior products. They are superior to competitor products, offer unique features that are most important to customers, provide excellent value for the customer (e.g., reduce total costs), and are of high quality.

B. Creating Market-Driven Products and Building in the Voice of the Customer

A thorough understanding of customers' needs and wants, the competitive situation, and the nature of the market is an essential component of new product success. A large number of studies prove that a strong customer focus increases success and profitability and reduces the time it takes to develop the product.

In-depth one-on-one interviews, customer site visits, observing the customer, and customer panels are examples of ways to gather valuable customer input. These inputs should become the key drivers for defining your product requirements.

You should share the product concept with the customers before development through mock-ups, prototypes, models, drawings, etc. As you develop your product, you should seek customer inputs (e.g., rapid prototyping, testing, and customer trials) throughout the process.

C. Pre-Development Work—the Homework—Pays Off

Successful product teams do their homework. They look carefully at competitor products. They see if the product is economically attractive. They define clearly who the target customer is. They gather customer feedback throughout the process. They know exactly what they need to do to develop a winning product.

D. Spiral Development—Build, Test, Seek Feedback, and Revise

Spiral development is a quick and iterative way to develop, get input, and make adjustments in shorter cycles.

E. Planning and Resourcing the Launch

Having a superior product does not guarantee that you will succeed. You need a great product launch marketing plan. These plans should be developed early on and refined throughout the developmental process.

F. Speed—But Not at the Expense of Quality of Execution

The first one to the market can gain a significant competitive advantage. However, speed is not more important than providing a superior product. The key is to shorten development time without compromising quality. Building in the voice of the customer, doing your homework, and developing your product in a spiral manner are some of the best ways to reduce your cycle time and, at the same time, improve your quality.[58]

ADDITIONAL CRITICAL POINTS

The following are additional critical points to remember as you begin to develop your product.

Position Your Product and Company as the "Original" and the "Leader"

Al Ries and Jack Trout, in their book *Positioning: The Battle for Your Mind* emphasizes that we live in an over-communicated world. We condition ourselves to take in so much information and then we block out the rest. So, how can you get into the minds of your target audience? The authors say that the easiest way is to become the first person. For instance, many of us remember that Neil Armstrong was the first person to walk on the moon. Most of us; however, don't recall the second person. Al and Jack emphasize that being original and the first in a niche is an outstanding way to position and brand your solution.[59]

Focus on Concepts that are New to Your Customer

People too quickly tune out when they believe they have heard something before—even if they haven't mastered it.

Become Likeable

Gallup reports that in over 60 years of tracking presidential elections, that *likability* is the most important predictor of outcomes for presidential elections.

Adopt a One-On-One Teaching Mindset

The most effective teachers connect with and help each person. We have been trained to write in the third-person. Instead, we need to learn to write in the first person. All of us appreciate more the teacher who connects with us and speaks with us one-on-one.

DEVELOP YOUR REQUIREMENTS

Determine What Products You Will Offer and in What Order

One of the first things you want to consider is what type of product or services you are going to provide that will help you to become a thought leader.

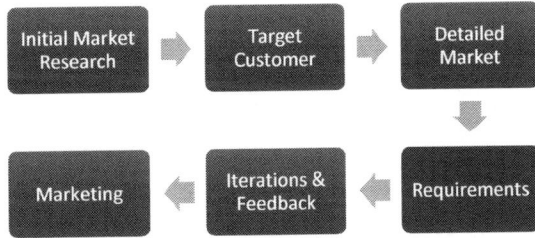

Initial Market Research ➡ Target Customer ➡ Detailed Market ⬇ Requirements ⬅ Iterations & Feedback ⬅ Marketing

Examples:

- Books
- Audio training
- Webinars
- Online courses
- Live workshops
- Membership sites
- Individual coaching
- Group coaching
- Consulting
- Mastermind groups
- Seminars
- Speaking engagements

Most experts make the mistake of selling only high-priced products and services. Providing various products at various price points, all focused on your niche expertise, can help you to more successfully generate business. When you offer products at a low price point to start, you provide an opportunity for others to warm-up and get excited about what you have to offer.

MARKETING AND SALES PIPELINE

- **Warm Up Process**
  - Free for Contact
    - Report, Tool, Introductory Webinar
  - Low Price
    - Book, Report, Webinar, Training Module
  - Standard Price
    - Online Training, Workshop, Membership, Webinar Series, Seminar, Tools
  - Medium Price
    - Coaching
  - High Price
    - Consulting, Mastermind Group, Do It For You, Software

crucial conversations
TOOLS FOR TALKING WHEN STAKES ARE HIGH

Public Workshop
Duration: Two consecutive days.
Cost: $1,195 USD

Trainer Certification
Duration: Two consecutive days.
Cost: $2,400 USD

Your objective should be to have a naturally growing pipeline of customers who understand what you can offer and are eager to work with you.

As you consider what type of products to offer and what marketing and selling approach to use, consider the next diagram. All the way to the left, you have your prospective clients or customers. Your goal is to collect contact information and turn those contacts into leads. Then, your goal is to

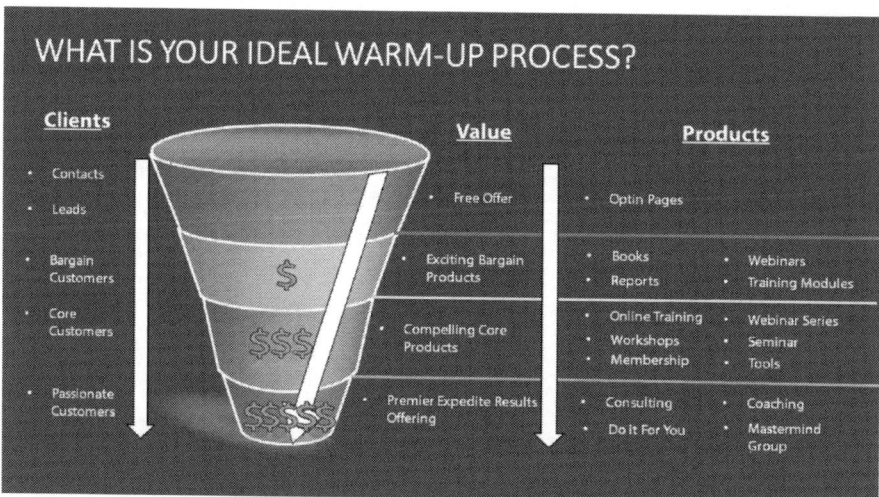

WHAT IS YOUR IDEAL WARM-UP PROCESS?

Clients	Value	Products	
Contacts			
Leads	Free Offer	Optin Pages	
Bargain Customers	Exciting Bargain Products	Books / Reports	Webinars / Training Modules
Core Customers	Compelling Core Products	Online Training / Workshops / Membership	Webinar Series / Seminar / Tools
Passionate Customers	Premier Expedite Results Offering	Consulting / Do It For You	Coaching / Mastermind Group

sell products at lower price points initially, with the hope that a certain percentage will become core or passionate customers—who pay more for your products and services. The column to the right provides ideas of different types of products you could offer at different price zones.

138

Begin to Define Your Requirements by Drafting a Sales Landing Page

Instead of starting this process with a traditional product requirements document, begin by creating a sales landing page. Why? Drafting a sales landing page helps you to become clear, from the perspective of the client, on the benefits you are offering. This approach ensures that your requirements are centered directly on the client.

When creating a sales landing page, keep your target customer profile in front of you to remind you of the customer needs and desires. Also, keep any of the documents you used to capture customer requirements on hand. Now, in the language of the customer, begin to draft your sales landing page.

A great sales landing page addresses the following:

- Who the audience is for the product?
- What is the problem or opportunity the product is focused on?
- Why this product is needed now?
- What the product is about?
- What benefits does the product provide the client?

The format and tone of a good sales landing page often includes:

- A captivating and compelling headline
- A description of the solution and how it addresses a passionate problem or goal of your target clients
- Visuals of the solution
- Video
- List of benefits
- An initial awesome offer
- A clear and easy way to convert call to action
- No distractions—so readers stay focused
- Testimonials
- A kind follow-up thank you page

We will review sales landing pages in greater depth in the next chapter.

BASIC PRODUCT DEVELOPMENT QUESTIONS

Audience

- Do you have a customer profile completed for your target audience?

Outcome

- What is the intended outcome for this product?
- How will you measure the outcomes?

User Stories

- What are the user stories for each audience segment? (User stories are short, simple descriptions of a benefit and feature that focus on the customer's needs or desires. They capture the 'who', 'what', and 'why' of a requirement in a simple, concise way.)

Marketing plan

- What are the key messages that will be delivered to your intended audience?
- What are the goals of the key messages?
- How will you connect and communicate with your target audience?
- What type of content will you create (e.g., text, images, audio and video)?
- What channels will you use to develop the messages?

Milestones

- What are the key milestones for developing your product (e.g., phases of development, initial launch date, future releases)?

Cost estimates

- What is the cost estimate to develop, launch, market, and maintain the product?

ITERATIONS & FEEDBACK

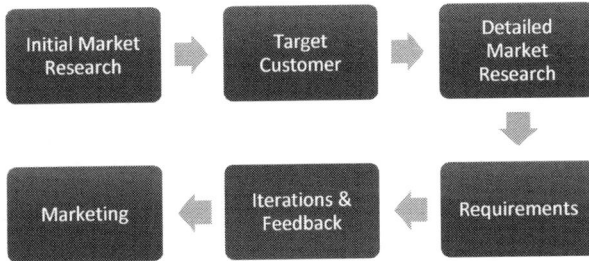

```
Initial Market      Target          Detailed
Research      →     Customer   →     Market
                                     Research
                                        ↓
Marketing   ←   Iterations &   ←   Requirements
                 Feedback
```

New products fail because:

- A superior product was not developed
- The voice of the customer was not built into the product
- No or insufficient market and customer research was conducted
- An effective launch and marketing plan was not developed and implemented

The Standish Group reported projects fail because of:

- Lack of user inputs
- Incomplete requirements & specifications
- Changing requirements & specifications[60]

Developing your product iteratively and getting ongoing customer input addresses several of these issues head-on.

BOOK TIPS

Typically, people start their knowledge business by writing a book. A book can begin to establish you as a thought leader. It is an excellent way to learn, clarify your thoughts, and develop a body of knowledge that you can use as a basis in your other products and services. It is also a lower priced product that helps to introduce you and the value you can provide.

HOW TO DISCOVER YOUR **PROFITABLE BOOK NICHE** THAT GENERATES BUSINESS

DAVID L. WILLDEN

One of the most helpful things you can do is to go into Amazon.com and see who the best sellers are within your category of focus. Become familiar with the books and the authors. Determine why they are successful and reading objective reviews can also provide insight. Often, the most objective reviewers are the ones who scored the book at a three.

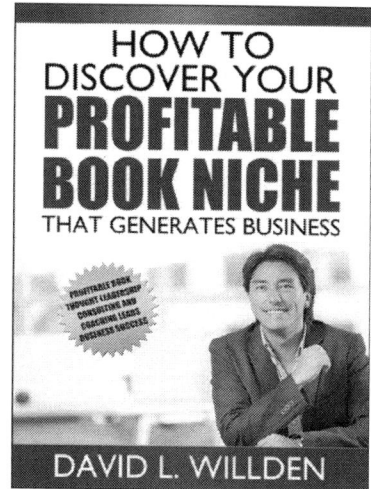

Remember that people are attracted to books that have attention grabbing titles and subtitles, captivating book covers, motivating descriptions, and large numbers of positive client reviews.

People typically purchase non-fiction books for the following reasons:

1. They are interested in biographies, current events, and history
2. They wish to improve their situation (e.g., employment, business, relationships, self-improvement)
3. They have a task or job to accomplish and want knowledge and guidance to help them

If you write a book focused on items 2 and 3 from above, the better you understand what your readers' pains and hopes are, what their hoped for outcomes are, and what holds them back, the more successful you will be. You can use this knowledge to start developing an outline of your book and to create titles for your chapter headings. An excellent way to design your content flow is to focus on the top pains or hopes of your reader early in the book.

Be aware of where other competitive or related books are coming up short. Where are the information gaps? What can you learn from the client reviews? Clients that provide three-star reviews often provide the most objective feedback. As you write your book, remember or learn about the four thinking and learning preferences that the Herman Brain Dominance Instrument identifies:

- What? (Facts): People with a "what" or "fact" thinking preference are most attracted to logical, analytical, quantitative, research, and fact-based information
- Why? (Future): Some people prefer understanding the larger picture and how everything fits together. They are typically conceptual, imaginative, synthesizing, and holistic thinkers.
- Who? (Feeling): These individuals are people oriented. They care about interpersonal relations, emotions, and communications.
- How? (Form): People with a "how" or "form" thinking preference look for how-to, step-by-step, organized, and sequential content.[61]

COACHING TIPS

Coaching involves helping a person or an organization achieve a desired personal, professional or organizational outcome. A coach may be someone who has greater expertise in an area and is there to help someone learn and master a skill. A coach may also be someone who is not an expert in a given area, but who is an expert in helping people to overcome barriers and succeed.

Relationship of Trust

Effective coaches understand how to build a relationship of trust. They assist the person or organization to understand where they are today, where they want to go, what holds them back, and what behaviors and actions are needed to achieve their desired outcome.

How to Discover A
PROFITABLE
CONSULTING AND
COACHING
NICHE YOU LOVE

Often, assumptions and erroneous beliefs hold people back. A good coach assists people to overcome these barriers often by asking open-end questions and discussing alternative approaches. They encourage their clients to set goals and work toward them and they are supportive and encouraging.

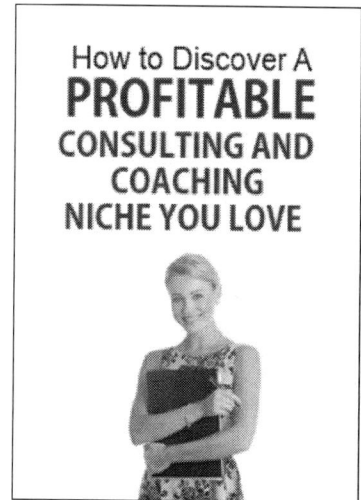

Marketing Your Service

It is helpful to understand that most of your potential clients are not actively looking for your services, even though they realize they have a need. Additionally, many of your potential clients don't realize they have a need. So, your marketing should not only focus on those actively looking for help, but they inspire, educate, and help these other two groups. Your marketing should help them improve and thus, feel better about themselves.

There are different marketing avenues you can use to help generate awareness about your offerings. Your website and/or your landing pages are some of the most important.

Offer an Introductory Session

An effective marketing approach that can help to develop a connection and trust is to offer an irresistible introductory offer. For example, you may communicate something like: "I'm offering a free 45 minute session on how to double your clients in 3 months. In the session, we'll get clear about the type of clients we are looking for. We'll review your current marketing approach and identify new ways to get clients. You will leave the session excited and eager to apply the new approaches so you can get the results you want."

Make the Introductory Session as Valuable as Possible

Make the introductory session as valuable as possible. Also, make this a positive experience for them so they feel good about themselves. You can do this by identifying and helping them to build upon their successes, talents, and strengths.

Work with them to develop a roadmap and action plan to move forward. Instead of trying to sell to them, offer to provide support to help them succeed. Let them know about a program you have that may help them and ask them if they would like to learn more. Don't be pushy. If they're not interested, feel good that you were able to serve them and help them to succeed.

LIVE WORKSHOP TIPS

A live workshop can be highly engaging and rewarding for both the participants and for the instructor. Below are keys developing a powerful workshop experience.

1. Determine the pain, aspirations, and needs of the participants.
2. Define how the learning will address these needs.
3. Outline the experience you want the participants to have.
   - How do you want them to feel about themselves?
   - What location would be ideal for your attendees?
4. Get to know the people before the workshop.
   - What information would best help you to serve them during the workshop?
5. Determine how you will engage workshop participants so it is a two-way communication?
   - Adopt a one-on-one and small group communication style. See yourself in the living room visiting with a group of good friends and use the same conversational approach.
6. Be a storyteller.
   - Continuously share memorable and motivating stories your participants won't forget.
7. Be organized and communicate that organization.
8. Give participants plenty of opportunities to practice, apply, and reflect.

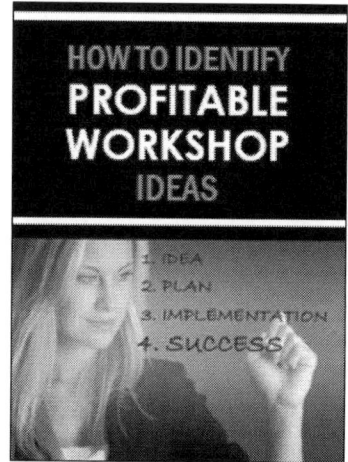

CONSULTING TIPS

Clients are looking for external expertise for several possible reasons. These could include:

- **Problems** they are confronted with and are unfamiliar with.
- New **markets** they want to focus on.
- **Approaches** or methodologies or standards they need help with.
- New **skills** they haven't developed.
- New **tools** they need help with.

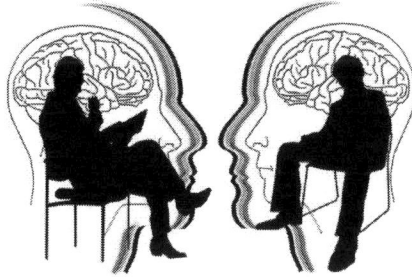

Be clear about which of the reasons you are focused on. Continually gather information to help you understand the pain points, aspirations, and tasks that your potential clients are focused on. Continually seek for new knowledge and insights that can help them.

If you are focused on problems, then articulate the various problems that potential clients could be dealing with. Clients care about outcomes. Identify the possible root causes and the ideal solutions for each. Continue to research and look for new ways to help your clients achieve greater results sooner.

If you are focused on new markets, then dig deep and understand the latest insights to helping potential clients succeed in new markets.

When you market your services, focus on selling results and not services. If you have to charge by the hour, then you will be seen as a commodity. That isn't what you want. You want to be someone that delivers high bottom-line value. Help your clients to understand the value of the end results. Help them realize that you understand how valuable you know their time is, that your time is also valuable, and that the speed of results is a top priority.

Develop a good system to constantly generate new business. As part of your marketing efforts, you will want to continue to grow your list of contacts and provide valuable information to pique their interest in you. Also, remember to always develop your case studies and testimonials so future clients know what you have accomplished.

Becoming a known expert and thought leader will expedite your ability to generate consulting business. So, this should to be a priority.

Remember that the more potential clients know about you and the value you can provide, the more interested they will be. Also, remember how important it is that you create good experiences for your clients so they can get excited and feel good about themselves.

WEBINAR TIPS

Webinars are an amazing way to share content, gather feedback, and create excitement. Some of the most successful marketing programs are webinar-based.

HOW TO DISCOVER PROFITABLE WEBINAR IDEAS

Popular Paid Webinars

Having a captivating webinar registration page is key to getting people to sign up. Your headlines need to be compelling and capture attention. You should outline a few points that the participants will learn.

When you conduct your webinars, be yourself, but let your passion show. Passion is contagious. You want people to feel your excitement for the topic.

A webinar is a visual experience, so use lots of diagrams and images and move at a fast pace. Some suggest that you cover one slide in one minute or less.

Focus on the pain, aspirations, and benefits. Help people to envision for themselves a better future. Use stories, case studies, and provide examples.

Share facts and research, provide step-by-step directions, and invite people to act.

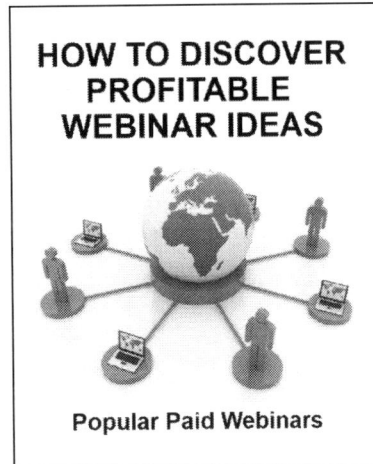

ONLINE COURSE TIPS

Start by developing an outline for your online course. Define the benefits the participants will receive from the course overall and for each section. Establish a learning goal for each section. Prioritize and sequence your content based on top pains or hopes, so your participants can early on connect, see the benefits, and get excited.

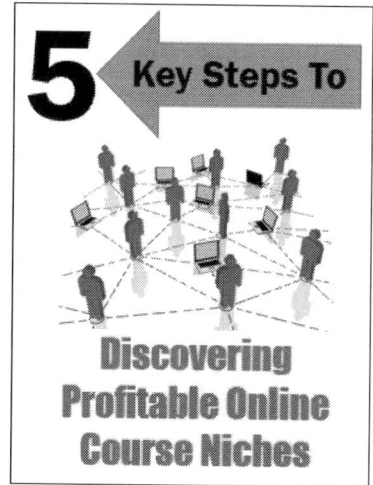

- Titles can capture attention and set the stage. Create titles for each section that include emotion words and speak to the desired benefit of the participant.
- Set the stage by sharing something that is unexpected.
- Share a story that evokes emotion.
- Provide facts and a holistic visual or diagram.
- Introduce new insights and explain the benefits of the insights.
- Remember to share facts, stories, and examples, provide directions, and build in exercises so that people can immediately begin to apply the knowledge.
- Present the information in a variety of ways. You could use pictures, colors, screencasts, video, and interactive content.

PAID MEMBERSHIP SITE TIPS

As you look at the human needs model, you can see many areas at all levels of need where a membership site could be valuable.

- **Basic Needs** (e.g., food, water, clothing, security): Discounts and tips on where you can save the most money. How to effectively grow and raise your own food. How to find and purify water. How to protect your family.

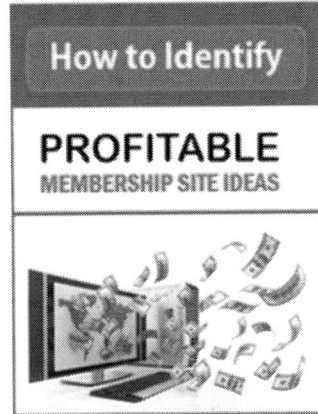

How to Identify

PROFITABLE
MEMBERSHIP SITE IDEAS

- **Employment**: Ongoing occupational training and education. Research data. Employment and contract opportunities. Networking events.
- **Health**: Most healthy foods, recipes, and diets. Exercise programs. Health tips. Access to health professionals.

A membership site needs to address an important pain or aspiration, teach people valuable new skills, show people how to succeed at important tasks, and provide other valuable information. Examples of different types of membership sites include:

- Training and education
- Best practices and innovations
- Discounts
- Data and analytics
- Research
- Source information
- Tools and software

MASTERMIND GROUP TIPS

A mastermind group is a group of members who meet together on a regular basis to:

- Learn new strategies and approaches
- Share best practices and lessons learned
- Develop relationships
- Promote each other's products and services

A mastermind group is usually made of 5 to 8 people. Often, these groups meet weekly, bi-weekly, or monthly through a web meeting. Also, the groups often get together 2 to 4 times a year in face-to-face meetings.

Key Ideas to Discover

PROFITABLE
MASTERMIND GROUPS

As a leader of a mastermind group, your role is to teach, facilitate, and help group participants to experience success. It is important that you as the leader are clear about the desired outcomes of each of the members. To gain this clarity, interview each of the members of the mastermind group. The curriculum and the set of experiences should be based on your interviews.

During the sessions, your focus should not just be on teaching, but listening. Focus on asking great questions. In fact, the quality of your questions will determine how successful you will be with your group members. When group members speak, take detailed notes. Identify what they said. Indicate what their reaction and emotions were. Your notes will help you to gain deep insights. Take the time to review and then reflect on the conversations so you can figure out how to best help everyone to succeed and have a wonderful experience doing so.

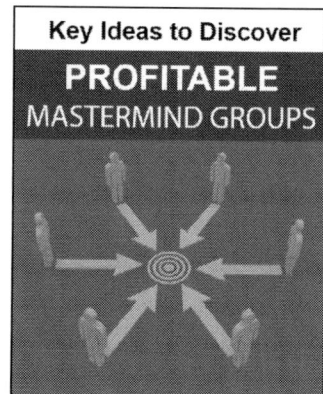

SEMINAR TIPS

Seminars are in big demand and that trend will likely continue. Seminars are opportunities for people to come together, get the latest training insights in a stimulating environment, and to network.

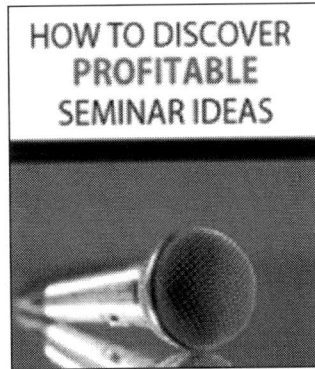

HOW TO DISCOVER PROFITABLE SEMINAR IDEAS

You want to choose a seminar topic that is something that potential participants would be passionate about, willing to pay good money to attend, and where there is a large client base to draw upon.

The most important key to seminar success is the reputation and quality of the speakers. If you understand your target niche well, you will probably have a strong idea of who the ideal candidates would be. If you don't and you want to save time, you could consider contacting speaker bureaus. Some bureaus specialize in specific target areas. A bureau will send you biographies and videos to help you narrow the selection down. If you don't plan to use a speaker bureau, then you will want to build in time to research presenters, review their content, learn how well they present, and check on their availability and willingness to present at your conference.

Where you host the seminar is important. Ask yourself, what type of environment would be ideal for seminar participants?

Where and how effectively you market will also determine your level of success. You will need to determine:

- Who the potential clients are
- Where they go now to get information
- How to best motivate them to attend the seminar

Having compelling and persuasive marketing content is vital to your success. Use a captivating and benefit rich headline. Be clear about how the seminar will benefit him or her. Include the Who, What, When, Where, and Why of the seminar. Include captivating large images and visuals.

There are several venues to market the seminar. A few examples include:

- Email
- Landing Page
- High Traffic Websites
- Joint Venture Mailings
- Third-Party Online Newsletters
- Post Cards
- Direct Mail
- Social Media
- PR Releases
- Paid Advertising

Typically, sign up rates are low for seminars, so make sure that you have a large number of potential attendees to advertise to. Extremely high rates are 1% for direct mail, for instance.

SPEAKING ENGAGEMENT TIPS

The most popular paid speakers are famous people (e.g., celebrities, top athletes, politicians, best-selling authors, CEOs). There are also some high-demand speakers who started speaking for free and began to develop a reputation. Chris Widener is a good example. "For the past 25 years, he has been working his way from 'free speeches to high schools and summer camps,' up to his current rate of $20,000 per talk."[62]

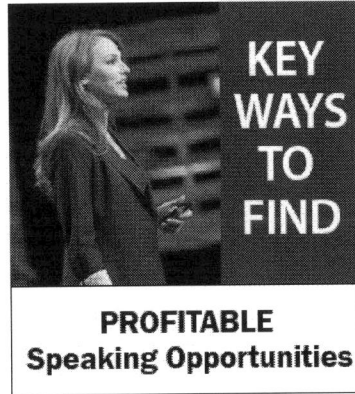

KEY WAYS TO FIND

PROFITABLE Speaking Opportunities

As you become a known thought leader, you will have greater speaking engagement opportunities.

AUDIO TRAINING TIPS

When most people think of audio training, they think of an audio book. There is a difference between the two. An audio book is simply an audio recording of your book. The price of an audio book is comparable to the price of a book. Audio training, on the other hand, is education-based. It is a course. It teaches a listener how to do something of value.

Audio training is ideal for those who want to take advantage of travel time, exercise time, etc., to grow and learn.

When you begin by creating an audio training outline, identify what the listener will learn and be able to do as a result of the training. Prioritize and sequence your content based on top pains, hopes, or tasks of your listeners. This will help them see the personal relevance of training and get excited early on in the training.

As you develop your audio training, remember to include new and exciting insights. Share stories and provide examples. Create exercises that help your listeners to apply and benefit from the new knowledge. Keeping the attention of listeners can be a challenge, even if you are a great teacher. Remember to provide variety and consider interviewing others.

9. How to Market Your Products and Services in Today's World

"Business is about marketing and innovation. Anything beyond this is a cost." Peter Drucker

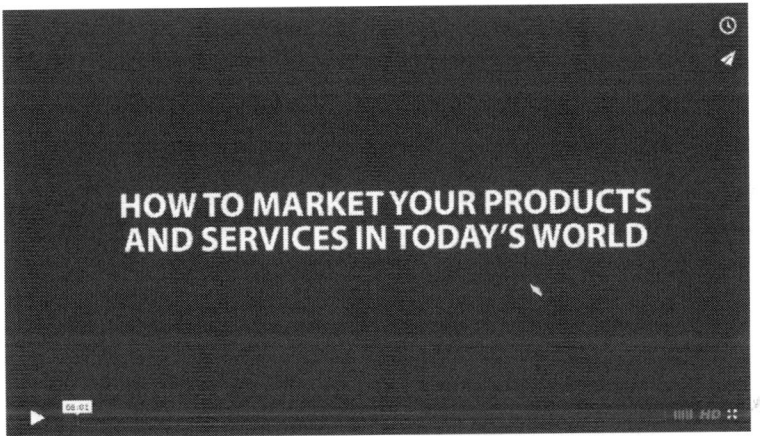

http://creating-you-inc.com/book-videos/

It seems that everyone is competing for "mindshare" nowadays. We are bombarded with content and messages. Attempts to capture our attention can be quite drastic. Even so, we have become quite effective in ignoring the noise.

So, how can you be successful in this world of sound bites? How can you create content that gets people to pause; to want to hear what you have to say?

Use yourself initially as a case study. Remember the last time you purchased something beyond your typical purchases (e.g., food, fuel)? Why did you buy it? How did you become aware of the product? What motivated you to buy it? Think through the last few purchases like this. What prompted you? What motivated you to pull out your credit card?

Now, look at your customer profile. Get into their mindset. The deeper you can get into their mindset and lose yourself, the more successful you will be. What would catch their attention? What would motivate them to cross that bridge from "free" to "buy?"

UNDERSTAND WHY PEOPLE BUY

"People forget what you said, they forget what you did, but they never forget how you made them feel." Maya Angelou

Emotional vs. Rational Buying?

Most of us believe that the buying decisions we make are based primarily on rational analysis and thinking. In truth; however, our emotions greatly influence and determine our decisions.

When we begin to make a buying decision, we draw upon our previous experiences and the emotions associated with those experiences. This is when we begin to tap into emotions. That is why people are willing to pay so much more for brand names. If you think about it, a brand is a mental representation in our minds. When we associate positive emotions with those images, we are more inclined to buy.

Motivation Insights

The Self-Determination Theory focuses on the motivation behind choices that people make. It is a well-established theory supported by ongoing research. It predicts that a person is happiest when three basic psychological needs are satisfied: autonomy, competence, and relatedness.

- **Autonomy**: A person feels autonomy when they make their own choices based on their own motivations and what is important to them. People want to be agents of their own life and they don't want to be acted upon or controlled by others.
- **Competence**: A person feels like they are competent when they can use their talents and ability to master a skill and create a desired outcome.

- **Relatedness**: Each person wants to interact with and be connected to others and they want experience caring for others. A person feels relatedness to other people when their activities develop supportive relationships and when a person feels understood by others.

As you develop your product, marketing, and customer interactions, focus on helping others to make their own **choices** by providing helpful information. Help them to truly become **competent** and to feel the joy of being able to create their desired outcome. Additionally, help them to feel **connected** and to better connect with other people.

Consider how Apple develops its products and marketing. They market their products in a way that makes people feel they are empowered and have more **autonomy**. They simplify and remove complexity in their products and provide additional, simple to use features that matter to people and that help them quickly become **competent**. They create a sense of community so people can feel connected and **relate** with each other.

Understanding Human Needs

Let's review the "needs of people" model below and identify for each need category (e.g., survival, security) what the key purchasing factors are for buyers.

NEEDS OF PEOPLE

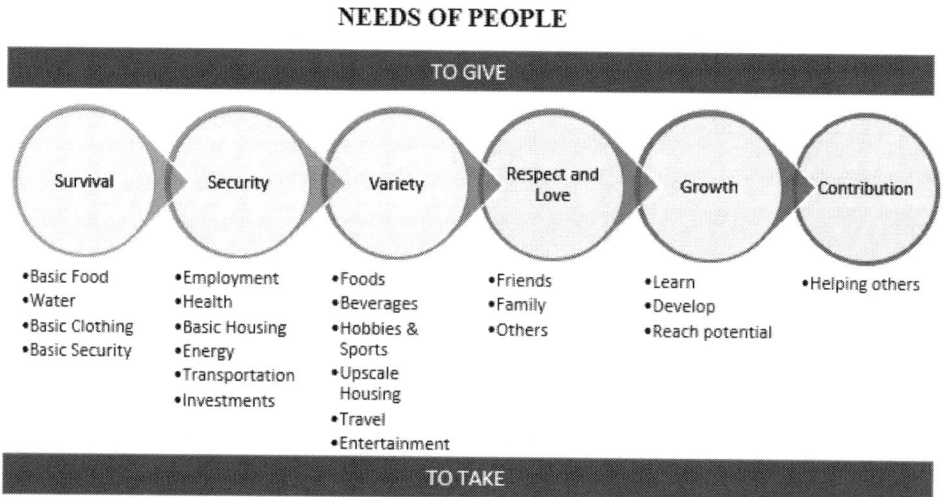

Survival

When a person has limited resources, they will focus on surviving. Their objective is to acquire basic food, clothing, and housing in a location where they can feel relatively safe. They are focused on finding the lowest prices at the closest location. Decisions are more rational than emotional at this point.

Security

Once a person begins to feel they have what they need to survive, their focus quickly shifts to stability. They concentrate on obtaining steady income (e.g. job, business), obtaining adequate housing, having the means to travel, and saving for the future.

Once a person begins to feel secure, their buying criteria shifts. Instead of just focusing on cost and location, quality and experience become more important.

Variety

People enjoy variety, fun, hobbies, sports, adventure, and a challenge. Depending on one's resources, cost and location considerations become less important and buyers look for experiences that best meet their interests.

Respect and Love

We all have a strong need for respect and love, even when we are in the most challenging of survival modes. Many spend fortunes on clothing, housing, transportation, education, training, etc. primarily so that others will respect them. These buyers are focused on style, quality, and prestige. For those who value love, having experiences together with family and/or friends becomes a high priority. These buyers are typically focused more on experience and cost.

Growth

People have a deep need to learn and grow. Part of the desire for growth is fueled by a need for security, variety, and to gain respect and love. The desire for growth can also be intrinsically motivated. Buyers here are looking for products and services (e.g. training, education, books) that can best help them to grow and feel good about themselves. Effectiveness, experience, quality, and cost are important buying criteria.

Contribution

The highest form of motivation for contribution is love or a genuine desire to help others find joy and to grow. Many contribute out of a desire for respect, love, and growth. Experience, effectiveness, and costs are also important decision-making considerations.

MARKETING—SUCCESS LEAVES CLUES

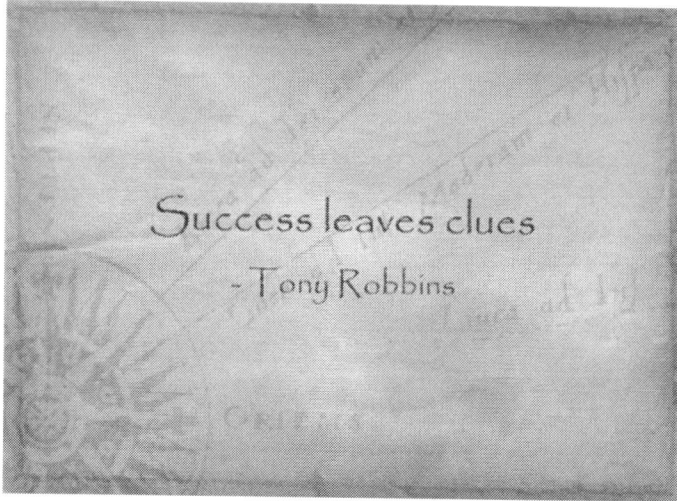

Success leaves clues
- Tony Robbins

What are the most important clues to marketing success today? Here are seven:

1. Marketing as Teaching.
2. Accurately Discover Physical and Emotional Needs.
3. Focus on All Who Need it—Not Just Those Who are Actively Looking.
4. Market for Response First.
5. Establish an Emotional Connection.
6. Organize Your Marketing Content Around Their Top Needs.
7. Design the Ideal Client Experience from Awareness to Service.

Clue 1: Marketing as Teaching

Most marketing functions within organizations spend most of their time and effort on promoting the company's products and services using selling-based messages. What they should spend more time doing is seeking to establish trust with their audiences.

As you focus on marketing, one of your top objectives should be to establish trust. Additionally, you should show that you understand your audiences' needs and that you genuinely can help them. One of the best ways to do this is to concentrate your marketing on teaching.

The objective of teaching based marketing is to:

- Provide value to your audience
- Establish trust and a connection
- Introduce the products and services you offer

Clue 2: Accurately Discover Physical and Emotional Needs

Those most effective people in selling are those who can most accurately discover what the greatest physical and emotional needs are of their prospects. The stronger the needs the prospect has, the greater the probability is that they will buy.

Prospects mentally have a list of important benefits they are looking for. If your product meets the most important needs they have better than other products, the greater the chance is they will buy from you.

Those most effective in selling will discover what the greatest needs are of prospective customers and speak to them. They also learn how prospects prioritize their needs. The higher the number of compelling needs you can discover and link back to the desired benefits of the prospects, the more successful you will be.

Clue 3: Focus on All Who Need It—Not just Those Who are Actively Looking

Those who have a need and are actively looking for your product are a minority of your target customers. This segment might represent 25% or less of your total prospects. There are also those who have a need for your product or service, but are procrastinating.

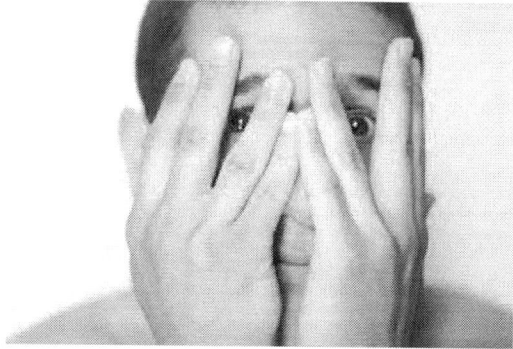

Additionally, there are also those who don't realize they have the need. These two segments may constitute another 50% of your potential pool.

So, how can you focus on all three segments: those actively looking, those procrastinating, and those who don't realize they have a need?

To those who are **procrastinating,** you may need a different marketing message. What headline will catch their attention? What images will awaken them to the need to focus *now* on the problem? What video and other content will speak directly to this crowd?

What about **those that don't realize they have a need**? Your marketing messages could be the same or it may need to be different. Again, what content would help this segment to understand that they have a problem and how your solution can help them to accomplish something or feel better?

So, consider *how* in your marketing to reach out to these three categories of people. You could possibly communicate to all three groups of people in your marketing pieces or you may want to create different marketing messages for each group.

Clue 4: Market for Response First

There are two basic marketing strategies that are used. One is referred to as branding. The goal of branding is to create a positive, emotional response when someone thinks of your company, products, or services. Creating a brand takes heavy investments and time. Nike, Apple, and Coca Cola are good examples of companies that have created strong brands.

The other marketing strategy is referred to as direct response marketing. The objective here is to evoke an immediate response and motivate prospects to take quick action. Direct response marketing approaches involve targeting a specific audience and speaking to their needs. It uses compelling headlines, images, video, and sales copy content. It also makes a specific offer.

Build Your Brand and Positioning As You Go

Although your initial priority will likely be to focus on direct response marketing, you will want to build and strengthen your branding and positioning as you go. Branding is the process of creating a name and image for your business and products that encourages buying and loyalty. Positioning involves attempting to claim a space and distinguishing your business and solution in the marketplace.

To establish a brand, you need to define what business identity or solution identity you desire and can represent. A brand includes a personality, so you need to define what personality you want to convey. Finally, you need to determine how to best convey your brand. To position yourself, you will want to define your target audience segment and identify how you will differentiate your business or solutions.

Clue 5: Establish an Emotional Connection

Studies have shown that creating an emotional connection with a consumer is more important than a psychological appeal.

In an article written by Dr. Peter Noel Murray titled "Inside the Consumer Mind", he shares:

- Advertising research reveals that an emotional response to an ad has far greater influence on a consumer's reported intent to buy a product than does the ad's content—by a factor of 3-to-1 for television commercials and 2-to-1 for print ads.
- Research conducted by the Advertising Research Foundation concluded that the emotion of "likeability" is the measure most predictive of whether an advertisement will increase a brand's sales.
- Studies show that positive emotions toward a brand have far greater influence on consumer loyalty than trust and other judgments which are based on a brand's attributes.
- A brand is nothing more than a mental representation of a product in the consumer's mind. The richer the emotional content of a brand's mental representation, the more likely the consumer will be a loyal user.
- Brand personality is communicated by marketers through packaging, visual imagery, and the types of words used to describe the brand.
- Another important foundation for a brand's emotion can be found in its "narrative"—the story that communicates "who" it is, what it means to the consumer, and why the consumer should care.[63]

Clue 6: Organize Your Marketing Content to Top Needs

Speak to the Most Important Needs First

Choose a specific audience and identify their most pressing or passionate pains or aspirations. If you generalize, you probably won't connect.

- *Magnify the Pain or Aspiration*. Remind or share with people how the problem or aspiration feels
- *Connect with Them*. To connect with them, start by referring to them. You can do this by using a positive and personal label that deeply resonates with the audience. For instance, the word "mother" has a warm, caring, nurturing feeling "Athlete" suggests that one is fit, coordinated, and has a passion for sports
- *Benefits to Results:* Identify the benefits in a way that helps the client see the results
- *Proof:* Provide proof. You can do this with your experience, client reviews, expert reviews, social media reviews, and comments
- *Urgency*: "Later" typically means never. You want to offer something compelling, quickly accessible, and applicable so that people take action on your offer. Examples:
  - To get instant access
  - You will get X results in X time
  - What is this costing you in lost opportunities?
  - Limited time
  - Limited products
- *Eliminate the Risk*: Provide a guarantee

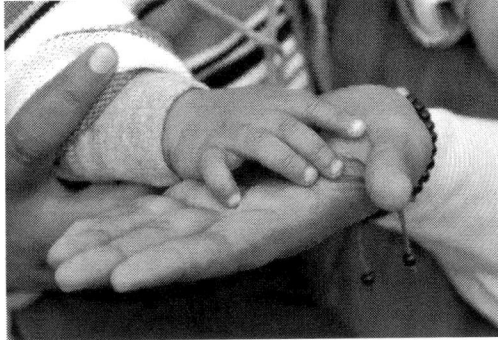

Clue 7: Design the Ideal Client Experience from Awareness to Service

Create experiences for clients that help them feel good about themselves and succeed. Here are questions to help you think this through:

- What emotions and results do you want your audience to have?
- **Awareness**: How can you create learning experiences for your audience that helps them to get excited, see results, and feel good about themselves?
- **Connection:** How can you establish a warm and friendly connection with them?
- **Purchase:** How can you help them to be excited when they buy the solution?
- **Success along the way**: How can you help them to be and feel successful in their journey toward results?
- **End goals**: How can you best help them to achieve their ultimate desired results?
- **Referrals**: How can you help them to become so passionate about your product that they will be eager to share it with others?

DEVELOP A POWERFUL MARKETING AND SALES PIPELINE

Important questions you may have are, how can you develop and organize your marketing and products in a way that:

- Captures the attention of your target audience?
- Motivates them to want to share their contact information with you?
- Encourages them to cross the bridge from 'free' to 'buy'?
- Helps them to benefit extensively from your products and services?
- Turns them into a passionate customer?

The next model can help. It is a highly effective approach that helps you to maximize your success. It works incredibly well for new experts who need to create a way for people to get to know the value of their work. It is also just as effective for seasoned thought leaders who want to keep their marketing and sales pipeline full.

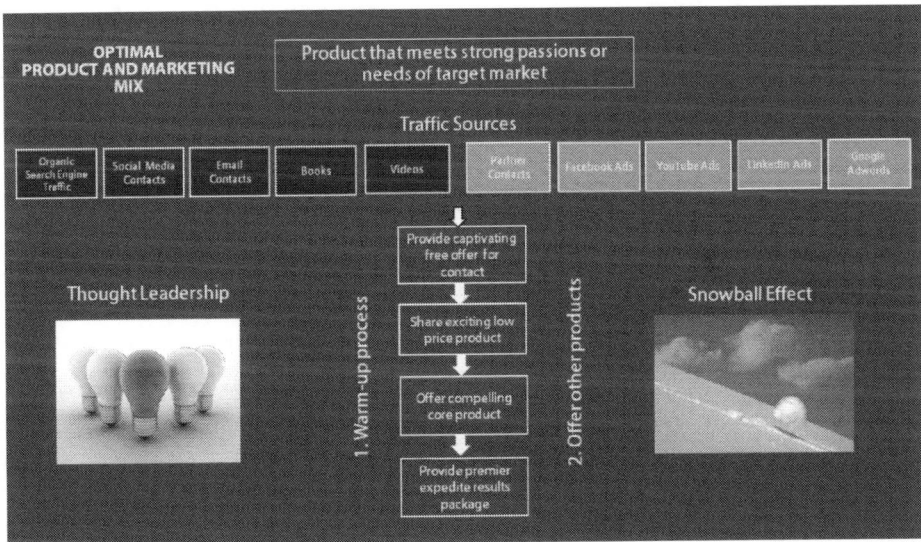

Notice "Traffic Sources" and the different channels that you can tap into to find prospective clients. In each of these channels, you can provide compelling, direct response content that motivates people to visit your landing page.

Just below "Traffic Sources" you see the box that says, "Provide Captivating Free Offer for Contact." Your objective here is to provide something of value that excites people and introduces your value—in exchange for their contact information.

The next box down reads "Share Exciting Low Price Product." Your marketing goal here is to provide a valuable product for a low price point (e.g. $7 to 9 dollars). This requires a financial commitment which is often a big hurdle. Once your customer pays for your product and finds immense value from it, they are more open to the value you can provide them with other, higher-priced products.

In your third marketing piece, you "Offer a Core Product or Service." The price of the core product shouldn't be too much of a drastic jump (e.g. over $500 dollars) because they still need to warm up to the value you can provide. In your fourth marketing piece, you "Provide (a) Premier, Expedite Results Package." Some of your customers will want expedited help and results and will be happy to pay a premium price for that help.

OPTIMIZE YOUR INFORMATION FLOW

Understanding how your target customers look for products and services and ultimately make decisions is key to your success. By understanding the "path" they take, you can provide the right experiences that ultimately help them to become a passionate customer.

So, what type of content and experiences should you provide to best help prospective clients learn about your solutions?

SMALL TO MEDIUM SIZED PURCHASE EXAMPLE

Consider the example below. This illustrates someone who will make a small to medium sized purchase (e.g. under $10,000).

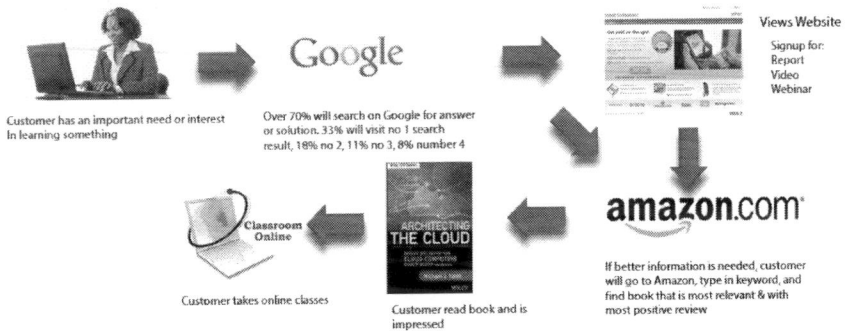

UNDERSTAND HOW YOUR TARGET CLIENT CAN BEST DISCOVER YOU

Example Small to Medium Size Purchase

Customer has an important need or interest In learning something

Google

Over 70% will search on Google for answer or solution. 33% will visit no 1 search result, 18% no 2, 11% no 3, 8% number 4

Views Website
Signup for:
Report
Video
Webinar

amazon.com

If better information is needed, customer will go to Amazon, type in keyword, and find book that is most relevant & with most positive review

Customer read book and is impressed

ARCHITECTING THE CLOUD

Classroom Online

Customer takes online classes

Let's say that an employee named Jennifer is with a division of a company that wants to offer services through the cloud. Jennifer is researching what cloud service models would work best for the company. She also wants to know who the best cloud providers are. To find the answer, she begins her search by going to Google. She finds a couple of online articles that you have written that are objective and insightful. On your site, you offer a report of the pros and cons of various service models in exchange for contact information. Jennifer completes the form and gets the report. The report is helpful, but she realizes the answer to her questions requires additional knowledge. She visits Amazon.com to see what she can learn. She purchases a book for $2.99 on the topic. As it turns out, the book was written by you. The book is extremely helpful and she is excited about what she has learned.

As Jennifer reads through the book, she learns of an online course that you provide. She signs up for the course and it equips her with the knowledge she needs to help her division succeed in offering their services through the cloud.

The COO of the company is impressed with Jennifer's results and asks her to help other divisions establish cloud based service models. Time is of the essence. With a bigger budget, Jennifer asks if you could consult with her and the company.

LARGER PURCHASE

The following image depicts the process that a person might go through to discover how you can help them. Purchasers are spending much more time on websites to get the information they need to make decisions before they pick up the phone to connect with you. Providing the right content in the right places on your website can help a person through the discovery process to ultimately make or recommend a purchase decision. When the company

UNDERSTAND HOW A CLIENT CAN BEST DISCOVER YOU

Larger Purchase

NEED	SEARCH	BASIC RESEARCH	DETAILED RESEARCH	PURCHASE BUY-IN	SELECT	PURCHASE
Customer has an important need	Customer uses Google to search and learn more	Customer researches features and results and prioritize	Customer narrows focus to see how your solution addresses their pain points	Customer secures buy-in from executive for purchase	Customer will narrow down to 2-3 vendors	

Awareness – informative, persuasive, engaging website   Details on website and live access

- How addresses pains
- Customer reviews / testimonials
- Basic features / benefits
- How address specific pain points
- Detailed features
- Comparisons
- Reviews
- White Papers
- Guarantee
- Simple processes and forms to expedite purchase
- Live access to person with answers

is ready to call and connect with you, making sure that they have quick access to a live person is important.

CONTENT AND DESIGN TIPS

Importance of Title, Headlines, and Photos

- People are five times more likely to read the headlines than read the rest of the content
- You only have a few seconds to grab their attention
- Your title, headlines, and photos are most important
- Most important headlines and photos should be at the top
- You can get noticeable results with photos. They can suggest a story
- On average, twice as many people read the captions under photographs than read the body copies

Design Tips

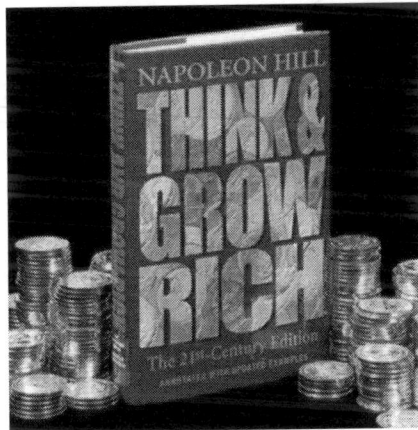

- The best designs are usually the simplest. The biggest mistake most of us make is to over design.
- The design should amplify the message and not call attention to itself.
- Bold your headlines and sub-headlines.
- Great designs inspire you.

Text Design Tips

- Bold headline
- Narrow columns
- Bullet lists
- Sub-headlines
- Captions under pictures

Font Style Tips

- Two font typefaces

- Two font sizes
- Two colors
- Align left

Visual Tips

- Visual hierarchy
- Picture equals half of page
- Title equals 1/10th of page
- Sub-headings = 1/5th of page

MAKE YOUR CONTENT STICK

As you develop your content, remember "SUCCES" from the seminal book *Made to Stick*.

LANDING PAGE TIPS

Your landing pages need to stand out. You have just a few seconds to capture someone's attention and get them to act. In those few seconds, you need to provide something that motivates them. You need to communicate your unique value proposition. You need to be likable and trustworthy. So, how can you do this most effectively?

Let's review the components of high converting sales landing pages.

- **Grab Attention**
    - You only have a few seconds to capture someone's attention.
- **Headline and Subheading**
    - Does your headline call out to them?
    - Does it focus on a painful problem or an aspiration they have?
    - Does your subheading further clarify or provide an additional persuasive message?
- **Image and Video**
    - People prefer visuals
    - Add a picture of your product
    - Provide a video explaining your product or service
- **Benefits**
    - Breakdown the benefits of your solution into bullet points
- **Call to Action**
    - Provide an awesome offer
    - Ensure your call to action stands out
    - Capture their contact information
- **Product Description**
    - Provide more details and images that answer peoples' questions
- **Testimonials / Social Proof**

Creating You, Inc.
The time is now to create your future.

NEW BOOK REVEALS

How You Can Create a Career or Business that You are Passionate About, Where You Can Excel, and Make a Real Difference

The working world will look fundamental different in the near-future from what it is today. We are just see seeing the tip of the iceberg of changes coming our way. Business and the economy will become significantly more global, innovation will become even more paramount to business success, and collaborative technologies will become commonplace.

With all of the changes underway, providing long-term employment opportunities will become more of a challenge for businesses. The need

Get Your Free Advance Copy

CREATING YOU, INC.
ENTREPRENEURSHIP AND CAREERS
HOW TO MAKE A REAL DIFFERENCE AND SUCCEED
IN A RADICALLY CHANGING WORLD

DAVID L WILLDEN

Get Your Free Copy Now
Free in exchange for Amazon Review

Free Advance Copy in Exchange for Amazon Review for .99 Cents

Let me offer you a free advance copy of my book so you can read it before my launch in a couple of weeks. Amazon is looking for reviews from those who have purchased it and won't allow me to purchase a copy for you. Consequently, in a couple of weeks, I'll

Landing Page Resources

LeadPages.net tracks which landing pages are most successful and provides landing page templates. It is an excellent resource. OptimizePress.com also enables you to use their landing page and sales page templates that are optimized for marketing and sells results.

PRODUCT LAUNCHES

You can develop an incredible product and still fail. Both innovation and marketing are the two key ingredients to business success.

Every year Schneider Associates and Sentient Decision Science LLC conducts the "Most Memorable New Product Launch" survey. The purpose of the survey is to look at how marketers introduce new products and what type of response they get. According to survey results, between 2012 and 2013, the top four most memorable product launches were:

- Windows 8
- Twinkies
- iPhone 5C
- Taco Bell

Windows 8

Microsoft introduced Windows 8 as cool and hip. They did this by introducing new, action packed music. They also featured young adults smiling and having a good time (e.g. roller coaster, para-gliding, surfing) and using the software (e.g. contacting each other, texting, using online maps, sharing pictures).

Windows used TV and social media channels to launch their advertising. Additionally, they opened up newly designed stores similar to Apple's.

Twinkies

The product re-launch of Twinkies was called "The Sweetest Comeback in the History of Ever." They focused their marketing on connecting emotionally with people. The launch was promoted in social media channels (e.g. YouTube, Twitter, Facebook, Pinterest, Google+, and Instagram.)

iPhone 5C

Apple held a press event to announce the iPhone 5C. They used billboards, street-displays, and television ads. Like Microsoft and Twinkies, they used emotional response based ads (e.g. people saying "hello" in different languages).

Taco Bell

In 2013, Taco Bell launched Nacho Cheese Doritos Locos Tacos and launched Cool Ranch Doritos Locos Tacos. They used a social media campaign to support the introduction. For instance, they promoted their videos on Vine, created a hashtag, and promoted that on Twitter. Taco Bell also produced a series of TV spots and posted them on their YouTube page. [64]

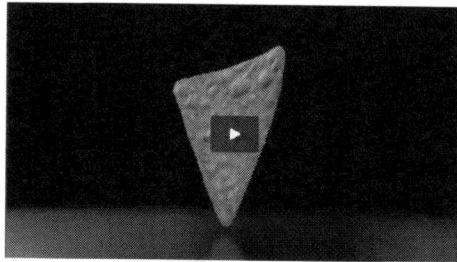

I would encourage you to learn about other top product launches by visiting: http://www.schneiderpr.com/launch-pr/most-memorable-new-product-launch-survey/

JEFF WALKER—PRODUCT LAUNCH FORMULA

Some of the most effective product launches I've seen were launched using approaches taught by Jeff Walker. Jeff teaches how to organize a sequence of exciting pre-launch content pieces. Jeff shows how to take these pieces to your audience in ways that create excitement and anticipation, demonstrate your credibility, help people to get to know and like you, grow your contact list, and demonstrate social proof.

Jeff emphasizes that when you organize a launch, you should build your marketing around mental or emotional triggers. Some of these mental triggers include:

- **Stories**: Nothing is more engaging than a good story. We love stories
- **Event-Based**: People love events and feeling they are part of something
- **Community**: When we are part of a community, we tend to adopt a group think perspective
- **Social Proof**: We often look to others for clues on how we should act
- **Scarcity**: When there is less of something, we instinctively want to get it before the opportunity disappears
- **Authority**: We are more inclined to believe and follow authority figures
- **Anticipation**: Anticipation can help to capture our attention and imagination. Anticipation is at the core of a pre-launch series that Jeff teaches
- **Proof**: People want to know that your product works. Show them that it does
- **Controversy**: If done correctly, controversy can intrigue us
- **Interaction/Conversation**: We often want to be part of a conversation instead of just listening to a lecture
- **Reciprocity**: When we give something to someone else, their inclination is to want to give back to us
- **Surprise / Unexpectedness**: We love a good and delightful surprise
- **Likeability**: We tend to buy from people we like and trust
- **Credibility**: If you are selling something to us, we want to know that you are credible

THANK YOU

Before you go; thank you for purchasing this guidebook. I'm anxious for your success. I would love your help. If you could take a few minutes to leave a review for this book on Amazon, I'd greatly appreciate it. Please click to access the book on Amazon to add a customer review.

Also, we invite you to consider taking a *Creating You, Inc.* workshop to accelerate your progress. To learn more visit—http://creating-you-inc.com/workshops/

Regards,

David Willden

ENDNOTES

[1] Crabtree, Steve, *"Worldwide, 13% of Employees Are Engaged at Work."* Gallup. Gallup Press, 8 Oct. 2013. Web, 25 Oct. 2014.

[2] Frankl, Viktor, *"Man's Search for Meaning."* Beacon Press, 2006. Print.

[3] Pofeldt, Elaine, *"What You'll Need to Know to Be the Boss in 2020."* Forbes. Forbes Media LLC, 3 Apr. 2012. Web, Oct. 2014.

[4] Williams, Ray B., *"The End Of Jobs As We Have Known Them."* Psychology Today. Sussex Publishers LLC, 9 Sep. 2012. Web, Oct. 2014.

[5] Erickson, Tammy, *"The Rise of the New Contract Worker."* Harvard Business Review, Harvard Business Publishing. 7 Sep. 2012. Web, Oct. 2014.

[6] Allen, James, *"As a Man Thinketh."* Gutenberg. Project Gutenberg, 1 Oct. 2003. Web, Oct. 2014.

[7] McCullough, David, *"1776."* New York: Simon & Schuster, 2005 Print.

[8] McCullough, David, *"1776."* New York: Simon & Schuster, 2005 Print.

[9] Rath, Tom, *"StrengthsFinder 2.0."* New York: Gallup Press, 2007. Print.

[10] Rath, Tom, *"StrengthsFinder 2.0."* New York: Gallup Press, 2007. Print.

[11] Rath, Tom, *"StrengthsFinder 2.0."* New York: Gallup Press, 2007. Print.

[12] Dweck, Carol S., Ph.D., *"Mindset: The New Psychology of Success."* Ballantine Books, 2006. Print

[13] Rath, Tom, *"A Quick Reference Guide To Strengths Basics."* Gallup. Gallup Press, Jan. 2007. Web, Oct. 2014.

[14] United States. *"Foresight and Hindsight."* The 9/11 Commission Report: Final Report of the National Commission on Terrorist Attacks Upon the United States. Washington: GPO. 2011. Print.

[15] United States, National Intelligence Council. *"Global Trends 2030: Alternative Worlds."* Washington: GPO. 2012. Print.

[16] Wikipedia contributors, *"Democracy Index."* Wikipedia. Wikimedia Foundation Inc.,

n.d. Web, Oct. 2014

[17] United States Department of State, Bureau of Educational and Cultural Affairs, *"Fulbright Fact Sheet."* Washington: GPO, 2014.

[18]Wikipedia contributors, *"Mikhail Gorbachev."* Wikipedia. Wikimedia Foundation Inc., n.d. Web, Oct. 2014.

[19]Wikipedia contributors, *"Democracy."* Wikipedia. Wikimedia Foundation, Inc., n.d. Web, Oct. 2014

[20]Lock, John, *"Second Treatise of Civil Government: Chapter 6."* Constitution Society. Concrete5, n.d. Web, Oct. 2014.

[21]Wikisource contributors, *"United States Declaration of Independence."* Wikisource. Wikimedia Foundation, Inc., n.d. Web, Oct. 2014.

[22] Wells, William Vincent, *"The Life and Public Service of Samuel Adams."* Volume 1. 1865. Print.

[23] *"Washington's Farewell Address 1796,"* The Avalon Project. Lillian Goldman Law Library, n.d. Oct. 2014.

[24] Karaim, Reed, *"Expanding Higher Education, Should Every Country Have a World-Class University?"* CQ Global Researcher. CQ Press, 15 Nov. 2011. Web, Oct. 2014

[25]Court, David, and Narasimhan, Laxman, *"Capturing the World's Emerging Middle Class."* McKinsey. McKinsey & Company, Jul. 2010. Web, Oct. 2014.

[26]United States, National Intelligence Council, *"Global Trends 2030: Alternative Worlds."* Washington: GPO, 2012.

[27]United States, National Intelligence Council, *"Global Trends 2030: Alternative Worlds."* Washington: GPO, 2012.

[28]United States, National Intelligence Council, *"Global Trends 2030: Alternative Worlds."* Washington: GPO, 2012.

[29] United States, National Intelligence Council, *"Global Trends 2030: Alternative Worlds."* Washington: GPO, 2012.

[30]United States, National Intelligence Council, *"Global Trends 2030: Alternative Worlds."* Washington: GPO, 2012.

[31]United States, National Intelligence Council, *"Global Trends 2030: Alternative Worlds."* Washington: GPO, 2012.

[32]Dr. Anthony Curtis, *"The Brief History of Social Media."* UNCP. University of North Carolina at Pembroke, 2013 Web, Oct. 2014.

[33] Business Dictionary, *"Smart City."* WebFinance, Inc., n.d. Oct. 2014.

[34] United States, National Intelligence Council, *"Global Trends 2030: Alternative Worlds."* Washington: GPO, 2012.

[35]United States, National Intelligence Council, *"Global Trends 2030: Alternative Worlds."* Washington: GPO, 2012.

[36]United States, National Intelligence Council, *"Global Trends 2030: Alternative Worlds."* Washington: GPO, 2012.

[37] Rosen,Evan, *"Every Worker is a Knowledge Worker,"* Bloomberg Business Week. Bloomberg L. P., 11 Jan. 2011. Web, Oct. 2014.

[38] Gertner, Jon. *"IBM's Watson is Learning its Way to Saving Lives."* Fast Company. Mansueto Ventures, LLC., 15 Oct. 2012. Web, Oct. 2014.

[39] Manyika, James, et al., *"Disruptive Technologies: Advances that will transform life, business, and the global economy,"* McKinsey. McKinsey & Company, 2 May 2013. Web, Oct. 2014.

[40]Manyika, James, et al., *"Disruptive Technologies: Advances that will transform life, business, and the global economy,"* McKinsey. McKinsey & Company, 2 May 2013. Web, Oct. 2014.

[41]United States, National Intelligence Council, *"Global Trends 2030: Alternative Worlds."* Washington: GPO, 2012.

[42] Alexander E.M. Hess and Thomas C. Frohlich, October 21, 2014, http://247wallst.com/special-report/2014/10/21/the-20-most-profitable-companies-in-the-world

[43]Bergin, Tom, *"Insight: Oil Industry Sees No Threat from Electric Car."* Reuters. Thomas Reuters, 1 Feb. 2014. Web, Oct. 2014.

[44] Hewett, Jackson, *"Financial Industry Ripe for Disruption Warns PayPal Co-Founder Levchin."* The Australian. New Corp Australia, 20 Oct. 2014. Web, 22 Oct. 2014.

[45]Berman, Saul and Marshall, Anthony, *"Digital Reinvention."* IBM.IBM Corporation, 17 Mar. 2014. Web, Oct. 2014.

[46]Berman, Saul and Marshall, Anthony, *"Digital Reinvention."* IBM.IBM Corporation, 17 Mar. 2014. Web, Oct. 2014.

[47] Bieck,Christian, Anthony Marshall, and Sandip Patel, *"Digital Reinvention: Trust, Transparency and Technology in the Insurance World of Tomorrow."* IBM.IBM Corporation, Feb. 2014. Web, Oct. 2014.

[48]Richards, Emily and Dave Terkanian, *"Occupational Employment Projections to 2022."* United States Department of Labor, Bureau of Labor Statistics. Division of Information and Marketing Services, Dec. 2013. Web, Oct. 2014.

[49]Richards, Emily and Dave Terkanian, *"Occupational Employment Projections to 2022."* United States Department of Labor, Bureau of Labor Statistics. Division of Information and Marketing Services, Dec. 2013. Web, Oct. 2014.

[50]Richards, Emily and Dave Terkanian, *"Occupational Employment Projections to 2022."* United States Department of Labor, Bureau of Labor Statistics. Division of Information and Marketing Services, Dec. 2013. Web, Oct. 2014.

[51] United States, Centers for Disease Control and Prevention, *"An Estimated 1 in 10 U.S. Adults Report Depression."* Centers for Disease Control and Prevention. Office of the Associate Director for Communication, Digital Media Branch, Division of Public Affairs, 31 Mar. 2011. Web, Oct. 2014.

[52]United States, National Alliance on Mental Illness, *"Mental Illness Facts and Numbers."* N.A.M.I. 5 Mar. 2013. Web, Oct. 2014.

[53]Ingraham, Christopher, *"Divorce is Actually on the Rise, and It's the Baby Boomers' Fault,"* The Washington Post. 27 Mar. 2014. Web, Oct. 2014.

[54]Holland, Jeffrey R., *"Are We Not All Beggars?"* The Church of Jesus Christ of Latter-Day Saints. Intellectual Reserve, Inc., 4 Oct. 2014. Web, Oct. 2014.

[55]Berger, Warren, *"A More Beautiful Question: The Power of Inquiry to Spark Breakthrough Ideas."* Bloomsbury, USA, 2014. Print.

[56] Drucker, Peter F., *"Management: Tasks, Responsibilities, Practices."* Australia: Harper & Row. 1974. Print.

[57]Kahn, Kenneth B., *"PDMA Handbook Of New Product Development."* John Wiley & Sons, Incorporated. 2004. Print.

[58]Kahn, Kenneth B., *"PDMA Handbook Of New Product Development."* John Wiley & Sons, Incorporated. 2004. Print.

[59] Ries, Al and Jack Trout, *"Positioning: The Battle for Your Mind: How to Be Seen and Heard in the Overcrowded Marketplace."* 3rd. ed. McGraw-Hill Companies. 2001. Print.

[60] The Standish Group International Inc, *"The Chaos Manifesto 2013, Think Big, Act Small."* VersionOne, Inc., 2013. Web, Oct. 2014.

[61] HBDI, *"Overview of The HBDI."* Herrmann International. 2014. Web, Oct. 2014.

[62] Clark, Dorie, *"How To Become A Successful Professional Speaker."* Forbes. Forbes, Inc. 10 Jun. 2013. Web, Oct. 2014.

[63] Murray, Peter Noel Ph.D., *"Inside the Consumer Mind."* Psychology Today. Sussex Directions, Inc., 2013. Web, Oct. 2014.

[64] Schneider & Associates, *"2013 Most Memorable New Products."* WorldCom, 2013. Web, Oct. 2014.

49811986R00103

Made in the USA
Charleston, SC
06 December 2015